# Write on Track

### A Handbook for YOUNG WRITERS, THINKERS, and LEARNERS

## Authors

**Dave Kemper, Ruth Nathan, Patrick Sebranek, Carol Elsholz**

## Illustrator

**Chris Krenzke**

## WRITE SOURCE®

GREAT SOURCE EDUCATION GROUP
a Houghton Mifflin Company
Wilmington, Massachusetts

# Acknowledgements

We're grateful to many people who helped bring *Write on Track* to life. First, we must thank all the students from across the country who contributed their writing samples and ideas.

Also, thanks to the writers, editors, and teachers who helped make this book a reality.

| | |
|---|---|
| Susan Ohanian | Candyce Norvell |
| Dennis Andersen | Stephen Krensky |
| Rebecca Davison | Allan Wolf |
| Charles Temple | Myra Zarnowski |

In addition, we want to thank our Write Source team for all their help: Heather and Laura Bachman, Colleen Belmont, Sherry Gordon, Beverly Jessen, Lois Krenzke, Ellen Leitheusser, Julie Sebranek, Lester Smith, Jean Varley, Sandy Wagner, and Claire Ziffer.

---

**Technology Connection for *Write on Track***

Visit our Web site for additional student models, writing prompts, multimedia reports, information about submitting your writing, and more.

**The Write Source Web site** . . . . . . . . . . . . <thewritesource.com>

---

Trademarks and trade names are shown in this book strictly for illustrative purposes and are the property of their respective owners. The authors' references herein should not be regarded as affecting their validity.

Copyright © 2002 by Great Source Education Group, Inc. All rights reserved.

No part of this work may be reproduced or transmitted in any form or by any means, electronic or mechanical, including photocopying and recording, or by any information storage or retrieval system without the prior written permission of Great Source Education Group unless such copying is expressly permitted by federal copyright law. Address inquiries to Permissions, Great Source Education Group, Inc., 181 Ballardvale Street, Wilmington, MA 01887.

**Great Source** and **Write Source** are registered trademarks of Houghton Mifflin Company.

Printed in the United States of America

International Standard Book Number: 0-669-48220-X (hardcover)

3  4  5  6  7  8  9  10  -RRDC-  10  09  08  07  06  05  04  03  02

International Standard Book Number: 0-669-48221-8 (softcover)

3  4  5  6  7  8  9  10  -RRDC-  10  09  08  07  06  05  04  03  02

# Get on the Right Track!

The *Write on Track* handbook is divided into five parts.

## 1 The Process of Writing

The first part will help you learn all about writing, from selecting a subject to checking a final draft for the traits of good writing.

## 2 The Forms of Writing

Would you like to start a journal, write a poem, or create a time-travel fantasy? Then this section is for you!

## 3 The Tools of Learning

Reading, speaking, thinking, and test taking are all important learning skills. They are all covered here.

## 4 Proofreader's Guide

Do you have questions about punctuation, spelling, or capitalization? This is where you can find your answers.

## 5 Student Almanac

Full-color maps, a historical time line, math tables—*Write on Track* is truly an all-school handbook!

# Credits

**Page 19:** From *Tornado* by Betsy Byars. Text copyright 1996 by Betsy Byars. Reprinted by permission of HarperCollins Publishers.

**Page 19:** From *At Home in the Old Oak Tree* by Sneed B. Collard III in IMAGES: BRANCHING OUT from HEATH LITERACY by Alvermann, et al. Copyright © 1995 by D. C. Heath & Company. Reprinted by permission of Houghton Mifflin Company. All rights reserved.

**Page 20:** Excerpt from *The Blue Hill Meadows* by Cynthia Rylant, text copyright © 1997 by Cynthia Rylant; reprinted with permission of Harcourt, Inc.

**Page 20:** From *The Lost Lake* by Allen Say. Copyright 1989 by Allen Say. Reprinted by permission of Houghton Mifflin Company. All rights reserved.

**Page 21:** From *Handle with Care* by Barbara Keeler in IMAGES: BRANCHING OUT from HEATH LITERACY by Alvermann, et al. Copyright © 1995 by D. C. Heath & Company. Reprinted by permission of Houghton Mifflin Company. All rights reserved.

**Page 21:** From *Boat Ride with Lillian Two Blossom* by Patricia Polacco. Copyright 1988 by Patricia Polacco. Reprinted by permission of G. P. Putnam's Sons.

**Page 44:** From *Thunder Cake,* Copyright © 1990 by Patricia Polacco. Reprinted by permission of G. P. Putnam's Sons.

**Page 213:** Copyright © 1998 by Houghton Mifflin Company. Adapted and reproduced by permission from *The American Heritage Children's Dictionary.*

# Table of Contents

## The Process of Writing

## The Forms of Writing

# The Tools of Learning

# Proofreader's Guide

# Student Almanac

# Why Write?

Why write? There are many good reasons to write. Writing lets you create stories, poems, and plays. It helps you learn and remember. Most importantly, writing allows you to share your thoughts and feelings with others.

*Write on Track* is loaded with ideas and samples of the types of writing you will do. It also has a special section called the "Proofreader's Guide" that helps you put periods and capital letters in the right places.

## A Big "Little Book"

*Write on Track* will also help you study for tests, learn about history, become a better speller, and much more. In other words, it will help you stay on track with all of your schoolwork.

Have fun using *Write on Track*. *Remember:* Something can be good for you (like writing) and still be a lot of fun!

Write on Track

A Handbook for YOUNG WRITERS, THINKERS, and LEARNERS

# Getting Started

# All About Writing

"There's nothing I like better than writing!"

Those are the words of Emily Martin, a student like you. Emily has more to say about writing.

Making up a story is like making a movie, and I get to decide exactly how it's done. I also like to write letters, thank-you notes, and happy-birthday notes. I like to write about my life and what happens.

## Writing Is Many Different Things

Emily says that writing can be fun. She also tells us that writing is a way to talk to others, and a way to learn about ourselves. No wonder Emily likes writing!

What else do you need to know about writing? Well, read on to find out. *Write on Track* tells you **all about writing.**

# The Writing Process

Writers like Emily use **the writing process**. You should follow the steps in the writing process when you write your own stories, reports, and other things. The writing process will help you do your best work—just like it helps Emily and other writers!

## Prewriting

- **Choose** a subject.
- **Gather** details about your subject.
- **Decide** what you want to say about it.

## Writing a Draft

- **Write** all of your ideas on paper.
- **Don't** stop to check spelling or punctuation yet.

## Revising

- **Read** and review your first draft.
- **Share** your draft with another person.
- **Make** changes to improve your writing.

## Editing & Proofreading

- **Make** sure that your words and sentences make sense.
- **Check** your spelling, capital letters, and punctuation.
- **Write** a neat final copy of your work.
- **Check** one last time for errors.

## Publishing

- **Share** your writing.
- **Display** it in a class or school writing collection.
- **See** pages 52-55 for other ideas.

# One Writer's Process

Peter Jones was asked to write a story about an event he will always remember. Here's how he used the writing process to complete his work.

## Prewriting

**Choose a Subject** ● Peter thought of two great story ideas—the time he broke his arm, and the time he raced in the pinewood derby. He decided to write about the derby because he had so much fun, and he remembered a lot about it.

**Gather Details** ● Next, Peter started listing details about this event.

- *my car ran great*
- *winning one race*
- *getting a trofee*
- *people taking photos*
- *my friends winning*
- *giving high fives*

After listing these details, Peter was ready to write his first draft. (Read it on the next page.)

# Writing a Draft

In his first draft, Peter put his ideas on paper. He didn't worry about writing a perfect paper.

I was in the pinewood derby and it was neat and I won.

I didn't win the first time. In the pinewood derby, they have a lot of different races. Every car gets to race more than once. In the second race, my car took off like a shot! And before I could say awesome, I won!

I got a trofee. Everybody congragelated me. I gave a lot high fives.

My friends Marcy and Eric won races, too. Cory won a trofe for best appearance. A guy took a picture of all four of us. I was kneeling down in front

When I got home my mom took another picture. I was holding my car in one hand and my trofee in the other one. Mom said the trofee was heavy. The picture was blury. I said it was okay. Then I felt really tired, so I went to bed.

## Revising

Peter read his first draft aloud to a partner. Then he changed, moved, and added ideas in his paragraphs.

**changed idea** ┈┈► It was one of the best days of my life.

I was in the pinewood derby. ~~and it was neat and~~ ~~I won.~~

**moved idea**

(I didn't win the first time.) In the pinewood derby, they have a lot of different races. Every car gets to race more than once. In the second race, my car took off like a shot! And before I could say awesome, I won! I was so surprised. ◄┈┈ **added idea**

## Editing & Proofreading

Next, Peter made sure that all his sentences and words made sense. Then he checked for spelling and punctuation errors.

My friends Marcy and Eric won races, too. Cory won a ~~trophee~~ trophy for best appearance. A ~~guy~~ photographer took a picture of all four of us. I was kneeling down in front.

## Publishing

Peter shared his story with his classmates. Later he included his story in a class book and added pictures to make it even more interesting.

### My Day at the Pinewood Derby

I was in the pinewood derby. It was one of the best days of my life.

In the pinewood derby, they have a lot of different races. Every car gets to race more than once. I didn't win the first time. In the second race, my car took off like a shot! And before I could say "awesome," I won! I was so surprised.

I got a trophy. Everybody congratulated me. I gave a lot of high fives.

My friends Marcy and Eric won races, too. Cory won a trophy for best appearance. A photographer took a picture of all four of us. I was kneeling down in front.

When I got home, my mom took another picture. I was holding my car in one hand and my trophy in the other one. The picture was blurry, but I said it was okay. Then I felt really tired, so I went to bed. What a day!

# Traits of Good Writing

Good writing has interesting ideas, clear organization, personal voice, well-chosen words, smooth sentences, and correct copy. Try using these traits in your writing.

**Interesting Ideas** ● The writing shares interesting information or ideas.

**Clear Organization** ● The writing has a beginning, a middle, and an ending.

**Personal Voice** ● The writing shows the enthusiasm of the writer.

**Well-Chosen Words** ● The writing has specific and colorful words.

**Smooth Sentences** ● The sentences are clear and easy to read.

**Correct Copy** ● The writing has correct spelling, grammar, and punctuation.

# Samples of the Traits

As you read books by your favorite authors, notice how pleasing their writing sounds. That's because they use the traits of good writing.

## Interesting Ideas

In the following passage from "At Home in the Old Oak Tree," Sneed B. Collard III gives many details about animals that live near an old oak tree. Naming each animal makes this information very interesting.

> As it grows, the oak tree gives food and shelter to an entire community of animals and plants. Squirrels, porcupines, and whitetail deer eat the acorns grown by the tree. Beetles, sowbugs, and spiders burrow into its bark. Earthworms, chipmunks, and meadow voles crawl underground among the oak's roots.

## Clear Organization

In this paragraph from *Tornado* by Betsy Byars, a farmhand describes the effects of a tornado. This short paragraph has a clear beginning, middle, and ending.

> I looked up, and I saw the sky. The ceiling was clean gone. There was the sky! The tornado had torn the roof off the kitchen and left the food on the table and us in our seats.

## Personal Voice

Your writing should sound like you! In her book, *The Blue Hill Meadows,* Cynthia Rylant's writing shows that she loves mountains and valleys and families with dogs. She knows a lot about these things, and she often writes about them.

> Blue Hill, Virginia, lay in a soft green valley with blue-gray mountains and clear, shining lakes all around. It was here that the Meadow family lived— Sullivan and Eva and their boys, Willie and Ray. And it was here that they found their much-loved dog.

## Well-Chosen Words

Choose your words carefully. Use active verbs, colorful adjectives, and specific nouns, as Allen Say does in *The Lost Lake*.

> I was glad when Dad finally stopped and set up the tent. The rain and wind beat against it, but we were warm and cozy inside. And Dad had brought food. For dinner we had salami and dried apricots.

## Smooth Sentences

Even though this passage from *Boat Ride with Lillian Two Blossom* by Patricia Polacco is about a rocky boat ride, the sentences read smoothly. Each sentence has a different beginning, and the paragraph has a variety of sentence lengths.

Suddenly the boat lurched, jerked, and heaved out of the water. Will dropped the oars and lost his balance, Banana Joe squealed, and Mabel tried to hang on. Then they all saw Lillian's face! She was young again.

## Correct Copy

In this paragraph from "Handle with Care," Barbara Keeler, like all authors, uses capital letters, commas, and quotation marks correctly.

The Tree Musketeers know that forest trees are important to the health of the planet. So are city trees. "They clear the air, make oxygen, cool the city, and muffle noise," said Tree Musketeer Alisa Wise.

# Writing with a
# Computer

A long, long time ago, writers used a sharp tool to carve letters in clay tablets. Later on, they used quill pens to write on parchment (an animal skin). Not too long ago, they used typewriters. Today, the most popular tool for writing is the **personal computer.**

Hi, *my* name is Travis.
I like writing with a computer because I can write faster and change things easier.

## Getting Started

Once you get started writing with a computer, you will see why it has become a writer's best friend!

I'm a personal computer–PC for short. From my monitor to my mouse, I am your personal writing friend. It's important that you know my basic parts.

1. My **monitor** is where you see your work.

2. My brain is located in the **computer** part. This is where I store information.

3. This is a **disk.** You can put it in my disk drive to save your writing.

4. You enter your writing on my **keyboard.**

5. My **mouse** doesn't squeak. But it does help you move around on the monitor.

6. You can print out a neat copy of your writing on my **printer.**

# Using a Computer

Once you know the basic parts of a computer, you can learn how to actually use it.

**Thinking** ● Remember, a computer can't think or write for you. You still have to come up with the words and ideas.

**Keyboarding** ● You need to learn how to type your ideas into the computer. (Turn the next page to learn more about the keyboard.)

**Word Processing** ● Practice using a word-processing program. It makes your computer work like a writing machine. First type a paragraph into the computer. Then add, change, move, or remove words. Check your spelling, save your work, and print out a copy.

**Exploring** ● Find out how the computer works best for you. You may like to write a first draft on paper, and then type it into the computer to make changes. You may also find that you like the speed and freedom of writing a first draft directly into the computer.

Remember to save your work often when you use a computer.

# Working with a Keyboard

## What is a keyboard?

The **keyboard** is your link to the computer. You use a pencil to write on paper; you use a keyboard to write on a computer See the keyboard on the next page.

## What do all of the keys mean?

Most of the keys are easy to figure out. Here are four of them you may not know about:

- Use the *tab key* to indent the first line of a paragraph.
- Use the *shift key* to make capital letters and some punctuation marks.
- Use the *space bar* to make a space between your words.
- Use the *delete key* to erase a mistake.

## How do you use the keyboard?

At first, you'll *hunt* for the right key and *peck* at it with a finger. That's okay, but it's not very fast.

Turn the page, and you'll see two strange-looking hands. When you learn how to keyboard, all of your fingers will be busy hitting the keys marked on each finger in the picture.

 You can practice keyboarding right in your handbook! To get started, place your fingers on the "home row" on the keyboard.

# Computer Keyboard

You can practice keyboarding right on this page! The hands on the opposite page show you which fingers to use on the different keys. To get started, place your fingers on the home row of keys. (The home row is the green row of keys.)

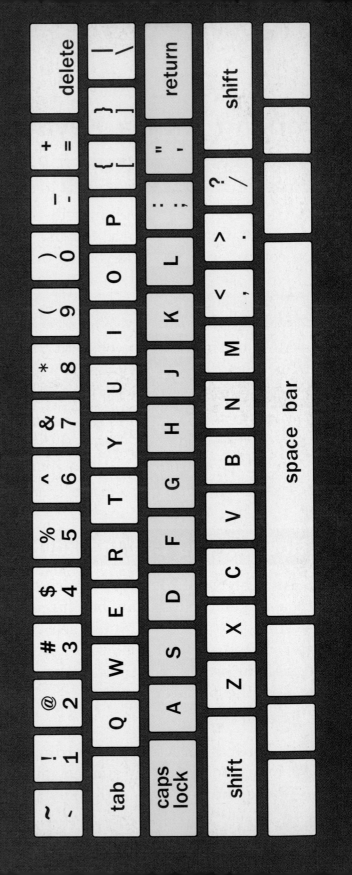

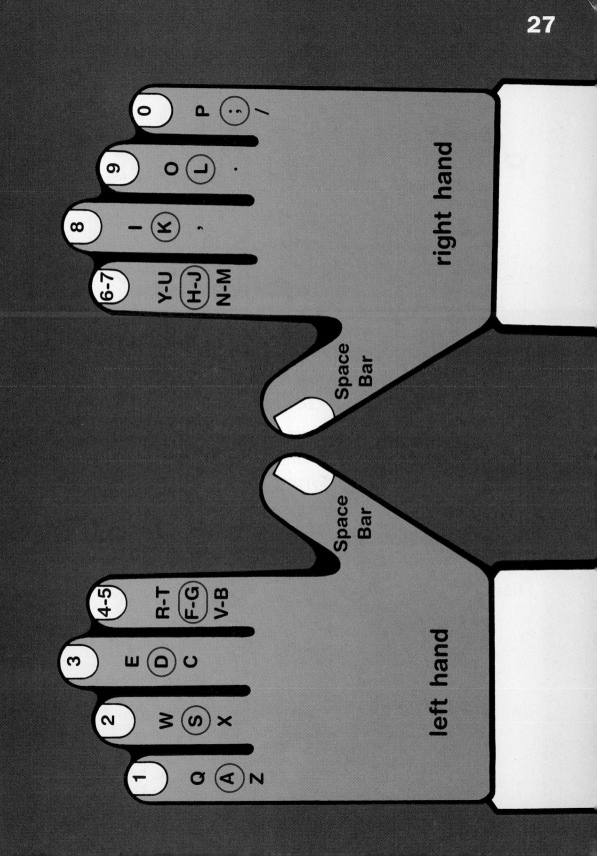

# Planning Portfolios

Jason Laws is a student who thinks that writing is special. He says, "Writing is a gift that you won't forget." Another student named Jamey Fleming says, "It's fun to look back at your writing and see what you did." Writing can be special to you, too.

## Collecting Your Writing

A portfolio is a place to collect your writing. In this chapter, you'll learn about planning a **personal portfolio** (just for you) and a **classroom portfolio** (for school). If you like writing as much as Jason and Jamey do, you may want to start your own portfolio right away.

# Making a Personal Portfolio

A **personal portfolio** is just for you. You can set it up in a three-ring binder, in pocket folders, or in some other way. You will want to divide your portfolio into different parts. This page shows a portfolio plan with four parts.

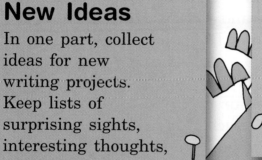

## New Ideas

In one part, collect ideas for new writing projects. Keep lists of surprising sights, interesting thoughts, new sayings, and so on.

## Writing in the Works

In another part, store your present projects. Maybe you're working on a nature poem or a true story.

## Personal Writing

In a third part, keep notes about what you do and things that happen.

## Finished Work

In a fourth part, save your completed work. The stories and poems in this part are ready to share.

"Writing is like a present to me.
Our class writes every day."

—Carl Thomason

# Making a Classroom Portfolio

If you do a lot of writing in your class, your teacher may ask you to make a **classroom portfolio.** There are different kinds of classroom portfolios. Two popular kinds are the showcase portfolio and the growth portfolio. Your teacher can help you decide which kind is right for you.

**Showcase Portfolio** ● In a showcase portfolio, you show off your best work. Your best work may include writing that you like very much. It may also include writing that you really worked hard on. Your teacher will help you decide which pieces are your best.

**Growth Portfolio** ● A growth portfolio contains writing you have done throughout the year. It shows how your writing has changed from September to December to May. By the time you get to May, you may look back at your September writing and say, "Wow! Did I write that? Can that really be mine?"

 Remember, there's a difference between a writing folder and a writing portfolio. A writing folder usually contains ALL the writing you've done. A portfolio is different. It contains only the writing samples you want to save or share.

# Portfolio Planning Tips

When you plan a classroom portfolio, follow these tips:

**Follow your teacher's directions.**

- **Know what your portfolio should look like.** Your teacher may give you a folder to use or ask you to design your own.

- **Know what to include.**
  Know how many pieces and what kinds of writing you should include. Also find out what response sheets you should complete.

**Be organized.**

- **Save all of your writing work.**
  Your teacher may ask you to include all of the notes and drafts for some of your writing.

**Keep up.**

- **Do each writing assignment on time.**
  Also complete any other sheets or work connected with your portfolio.

- **Do your best work from start to finish.**
  Keep everything neat and organized.

Ask for help when you have a question about your portfolio or about a writing assignment. It's important that you stay on track with all of your work.

# Prewriting and Drafting Guide

# Choosing a Subject

Sometimes, the hardest part of writing is finding a subject to write about. It's a lot easier if you build a file of writing ideas. To get started, you have to think and act like a writer. That means you must always be on the lookout for interesting subjects.

When you see or hear something unusual or important, write it down. Just write it down!

## Keeping a Notebook!

Keep all of your ideas in a notebook, where they'll be ready for your next writing assignment. This chapter lists a number of ways to build a file of writing ideas.

# Look, Listen, and Learn

 **Keep your eyes open.**

Sometimes a subject finds you! You might look up and see a hawk. You wonder about it. Where does it live? What does it eat? Write this subject in your notebook, along with a few questions.

 **Draw a life map.**

Put in important events in your life. Start with the day you were born. Then check your map when you need a writing idea.

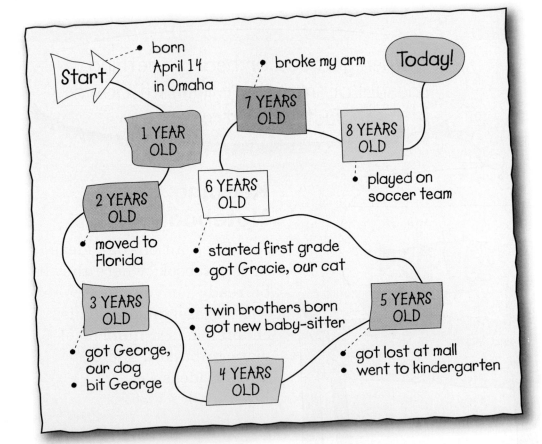

Start

born
April 14
in Omaha

broke my arm

Today!

7 YEARS OLD

1 YEAR OLD

8 YEARS OLD

6 YEARS OLD

played on soccer team

2 YEARS OLD

moved to Florida

started first grade
got Gracie, our cat

3 YEARS OLD

twin brothers born
got new baby-sitter

5 YEARS OLD

got George, our dog
bit George

4 YEARS OLD

got lost at mall
went to kindergarten

### Make a list of your bests, worsts, and favorites.

Here are a few ideas to get you started:

**Bests:**    My best days
My best friends
The things I'm best at

**Worsts:**    My worst subject
My least favorite chores
My dumbest moments

**Favorites:**    My favorite books
My favorite animals
My favorite places

### Read a lot.

Read books and magazines. Search the Internet. Read about things you've never read about before—the solar system, raising rabbits, and so on. Jot down writing ideas as you read.

### Do a lot.

Try new things. Join new clubs. Make new friends. The more you do, the more you'll have to write about.

### Write often.

In a journal (or in your idea notebook), write about things you see, hear, and do. Remember to check your journal or notebook when you need a subject to write about.

# Gathering Details

Once you've chosen a subject to write about, you need to collect and organize details. **Details** are the facts and ideas that make your writing interesting.

## Gathering Strategies

Here are three ways to collect details for your writing:

- **Find facts** from books, newspapers, the Internet, magazines, videos, and CD's.

- **Talk to other people** about your subject. (See "Learning to Interview," pages 252-255, for help.)

- **Gather your thoughts.** Some writers call this brainstorming. On the next page, we list several ways to gather and organize your thoughts.

# Organizing Details

As you gather your details, here are some ways to organize them.

**List ideas.** Listing is one of the easiest ways to gather and organize your ideas. Just write your subject at the top of a piece of paper. Then start listing ideas as they come to mind. Later you can put them in order.

**Answer the 5 W's.** Answer these five questions—*Who? What? When? Where?* and *Why?*

**Make a cluster or map.** Clustering, or mapping, is a good way to think about a subject. Clustering helps you organize the ideas that pop into your head. (See page 264 for a sample cluster.)

**Use a collection sheet.** Collection sheets and gathering grids help you gather and keep track of your ideas. (See page 138 for a sample grid.)

Answer these questions before you write your first draft.

**Subject:** Who or what are you writing about?
**Purpose:** Why are you writing? To tell a story? To explain?
**Form:** Will you write a report? A story? A letter?
**Audience:** Who will read your writing?
**Voice:** Should your writing sound friendly? Serious? Funny?

# Writing a First Draft

When you've picked a subject, chosen a form, and collected lots of ideas, it's time to write your first draft.

## Write Your Beginning

The **beginning** has to tell what you are writing about, and it has to make your readers want to keep reading. Here are some ways to write your first sentence:

**A Surprising Fact**
In one German city, passengers can ride a 100-year-old monorail.

**A Quotation**
"Riding a monorail can save time and money," said the mayor.

**A Question**
Could monorails solve our city's traffic and parking problems?

 **TIP** You can complete the beginning part with other details that support your first sentence.

## Write the Middle Part

The **middle** part of your writing should include more facts and details about your subject. Here is a middle paragraph that describes a monorail.

> Monorails are trains that run on one rail. Monorails get their power from electricity or gas. They are quiet and take up very little space.

 If you get stuck writing the middle, try telling someone else about your subject. Then write down the details and ideas you shared. You don't need to have a perfect paper at this time.

## Write the Ending

For the **ending**, remind your readers about your main idea, or give them something more to think about.

> Many amusement parks use monorails to carry people from place to place. I think our city should use monorails to carry people and to help solve our traffic problems!

When you have written down all of your ideas, your first draft is done. Good for you! (See page 15 for a sample first draft.)

# Revising and Editing Guide

# Revising
## Your Writing

Do you remember Pinocchio, the puppet built by the wood-carver Geppetto? Geppetto cut the wood with care, chiseled here, and sanded there. Finally, Pinocchio looked like a real boy, and actually came to life!

### Making Your First Draft Better

As a writer, you are like a wood-carver. You make big changes and little changes until your writing is clear, complete, and interesting.

When you take the time to **revise** your writing and bring it to life, you will have something to be proud of—as Geppetto was proud of Pinocchio.

# Improving Your First Draft

 **Read your draft to yourself.**

When you're ready to revise, read your first draft two or three times.

- Read it out loud once to get the main idea.
- Then read it again to see if it sounds good.
- As you read, listen for parts that you like and parts that need work. (Put a check ✔ by the parts you need to fix.)

 **Share your draft with others.**

Your friends and classmates may have good ideas you didn't think of.

- Ask them which parts they like.
- Ask them which parts they have questions about.

 **Check your organization.**

Does your writing have a good beginning, middle, and ending? (See the next page for help.)

 **Review your sentences.**

Are your sentences smooth and easy to read?

**Check your words.**

Does your writing include a lot of specific and interesting words? (See page 44 for help.)

# Checking Your Organization

## Beginning

Make sure the beginning introduces or names your subject in an interesting way.

**One way:** Let's get a monorail.

**A better way: Could monorails solve our city's traffic and parking problems? The mayor set up a committee to see how monorails work in Tokyo and Sydney. The committee believes monorails could work well in our city.**

## Middle

Make sure the middle part describes or tells about your subject.

**Monorails can be built over freeways in crowded cities. Most monorails get their power from electricity, so they cause less pollution. They move people quickly and quietly.**

## Ending

Make sure the ending reminds your readers about the subject.

**One way:** That is all I have to say about monorails.

**A better way: Some amusement parks and large cities have monorails to move people from place to place. I think our city needs a monorail to carry people and to solve our traffic problems.**

# Bringing Your Writing to Life

**Show, don't tell.** One of the best ways to bring your writing to life is to "show" instead of "tell."

**Telling:** We had a neat fort. *(Ho-hum.)*

**Showing:** **Our fort stood on stilts six feet high! The floor was covered with old carpet samples and looked like a crazy checkerboard.** *(Yes!)*

**Use the five senses.** The authors below used details that help you to see and smell a field of wildflowers and to hear and feel a thunderstorm.

> Wildflowers, the colors of the rainbow, danced on the hillside. The air smelled like sunshine and spices.
>
> — Joy Woods

> When the thunder ROARED above us so hard it shook the windows and rattled the dishes in the cupboards, we just smiled and ate our Thunder Cake.
>
> — Patricia Polacco, *Thunder Cake*

# Revising Checklist

✔ Ideas

___ **Does my writing make sense?**

___ **Do I need to add any ideas or details?**

___ **Do I need to cut information that is off the subject?**

✔ Organization

___ **Does my writing have a good beginning?**

___ **Do I need to move any information to a new place?**

___ **Does my writing have a good ending?**

✔ Personal Voice

___ **Do I sound like I care about my subject?**

✔ Words and Sentences

___ **Are my words specific and interesting?**

___ **Are my sentences smooth and easy to read?**

# Working with
# Partners

Dentists talk about strong teeth; bus drivers talk about safety. When people who have the same job get together to talk, it's called a meeting or a conference. People share ideas in order to do their jobs better.

You can hold a meeting to share ideas about your writing. Maybe you'd like to talk with one other person or with a small group. Your goal is to help one another do your best work.

Writing partners can help you see the strongest parts of your writing, get new ideas, fix problems, and find mistakes.

# When to Work with Partners

You can work with partners during different steps in the writing process.

## During Prewriting

**Partners can help you . . .**
- choose a subject to write about, and
- think of places to find information.

## After Your First Draft

**Partners can tell you . . .**
- what they like, and
- what parts are unclear or out of order.

## As You Revise

**Partners can tell you if . . .**
- your beginning gets their interest,
- your middle sticks to the subject, and
- your ending is strong.

## As You Edit and Proofread

**Partners can help you . . .**
- find sentence errors,
- choose the right words to use, and
- correct punctuation and spelling errors.

# How to Work with Partners

## When You're the Writer

- **Have your writing ready to share.** You can share your writing at different times during the writing process.

- **Tell your partners something about your writing.** (But don't say too much.)

- **Read your writing aloud.**

- **Listen to what your partners say about it.** (You may not always agree with them, but take time to think about what they say.)

## When You're the Listener

- **Listen carefully to the writer.**

- **Jot down a few notes to help you remember ideas.**

- **Tell the writer something you like about the writing.** ("I like the way . . . .")

- **Ask about things you don't understand.** ("What do you mean when you say . . . ?")

- **Be kind.** Always talk about the writing in a helpful way. (Say something like this: "Maria, I don't think *ran* is the best word for what that dog did. How about *charged*?")

# Using a Response Sheet

You can use a **response sheet** when you work with partners. It can help you make comments about a partner's writing.

## Response Sheet

✔ **Ideas**

___ **Does the writing have interesting information or ideas?**

___ **Are there enough details and examples?**

✔ **Organization**

___ **Does the writing have a beginning, a middle, and an ending?**

___ **Are all of the ideas related to the subject of the writing?**

✔ **Sentences**

___ **Are the sentences easy to read?**

✔ **Correct Copy**

___ **Is the writing free of spelling and punctuation errors?**

___ **Are capital letters used for names and for beginnings of sentences?**

# Editing and Proofreading

**Editing** and **proofreading** help you get your writing ready to share. After you have changed, or revised, the main ideas in your first draft, you need to edit your writing. Editing means making sure that your writing is clear and correct. Then you need to proofread. Proofreading means checking for errors one last time before you share a final copy.

## Asking for Help

It is easy to miss errors when you edit and proofread. So make sure that you ask a classmate, a teacher, or a family member to help you. All writers, even your favorite authors, get help during this final step in the process.

# Editing and Proofreading

## ✔ Sentences

___ **Are all of my sentences complete?**
(See pages 72-73 for help.)

___ **Could some of my sentences be longer?**
(See page 75.)

## ✔ Words

___ **Have I used the right words (*one* instead of *won*)?**
(See pages 316-321 for help.)

___ **Have I spelled my words correctly?**
(See pages 312-315.)

## ✔ Punctuation and Capitalization

___ **Have I put the right end punctuation mark after each sentence?**
(See pages 294, 301, and 302.)

___ **Have I capitalized names and the first word of each sentence?**
(See pages 305-307 for help.)

# Publishing
## Your Writing

**Publishing** is the last step in the writing process. It means sharing one of your poems, stories, plays, or letters. Amy L. George is a student writer who loves this step in the process.

> The writing process is like a birthday party. When the party is over, I share my favorite presents, my stories.

## Making Contact

Reading your story to your classmates is one way to publish. Putting your poem on a class bulletin board is another way. There are many other exciting ways to publish your best writing. You can learn about some of them on the next three pages.

Snow

It snow

so school le

# Five Great Publishing Ideas

## Send It!

- Mail a family story or a special poem to a relative.
- Fax an adventure story to a friend who has just moved.
- E-mail a story to a friend.
- Send a fan letter to someone you admire.
- Write a letter to a company or a public office asking for information.

## Act It Out!

- Act out one of your plays with the help of your classmates.
- Perform one of your stories or poems. (See pages 238-243 for guidelines for performing a poem.)
- Tape-record or videotape your story so faraway friends and relatives can enjoy it.
- Read one of your best pieces of writing to a parent-teacher group.

## Print It!

- Put together a book of your own stories or poems. Or make a class book. (See the next page for help.)
- Print a class newspaper.
- Make copies of book reviews for the school library.
- Create a picture book for younger students.
- Fax a poem to a family member.

## Submit It!

The magazines and Web sites listed below publish student stories, poems, and letters. Send your best work to the editor. When you are sending something to a magazine, include a self-addressed stamped envelope for a reply. (Ask your teacher for help.)

*Highlights for Children*
Children's Mail
803 Church Street
Honesdale, PA 18431

*KidNews*
(on-line publishing)
<www.kidnews.com>

*Midlink*
(on-line publishing)

*Stone Soup*
PO Box 83
Santa Cruz, CA 95063

## Bind It!

Make your own book by following these steps:

**1** Put your writing together in the best order.

**2** Staple or sew the pages together.

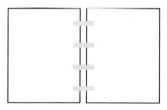

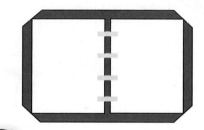

**3** For a cover, cut two pieces of cardboard to the right size. Tape them together.

**4** Place the cardboard on contact paper or cloth. Turn the edges of this material over the cardboard.

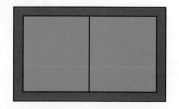

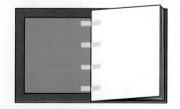

**5** Glue pieces of paper to the inside of the cover.

**6** Tape the pages into the cover. (Cover the tape.)

# Writing Paragraphs

# Writing
# Paragraphs

Where does every good sentence belong? It belongs in a good paragraph, of course. A **paragraph** is made up of several sentences, all about the same subject. If you put these sentences together in just the right way, they will present a clear and interesting picture of your subject.

## Learning About Paragraphs

In this chapter, you will find out about the basic parts of a paragraph, the different kinds of paragraphs, and the steps in the paragraph-writing process.

# The Basic Parts of a Paragraph

Most paragraphs have three parts. The first part is the **topic sentence.** It gives the main idea of the paragraph. The **body** or middle part explains or describes the main idea. The **closing sentence** reminds readers what the paragraph is about. Here's how these three parts make a paragraph.

**1**

Topic
sentence

**2**

Body

**3**

Closing
sentence

Snow Day!

It snowed a lot yesterday, so school let out early. It started to snow before lunch. At first, a few big flakes came floating down. Then it came down harder and harder. Snow piled up on the playground. At 12:30, the principal announced that school would let out at 1:00. Thanks to the snowstorm, we had a free afternoon!

# A Closer Look at the Parts

**1** **The Topic Sentence** ● A good topic sentence does two things: (1) It names the subject. (2) It tells what part of the subject you will talk about. (The part of a subject you talk about is called the *focus.*)

> It snowed a lot yesterday **(subject)**, so school let out early **(focus)**.

**2** **The Body** ● The sentences in the body explain or describe the subject. All of the ideas in the body should be stated in the best order. To help put things in order, make a list of the main ideas *before* you write your paragraph.

> It started to snow.
> – Big flakes fell at first.
> – Snow piled up.
> – The principal closed school early.

**3** **The Closing Sentence** ● The last sentence reminds readers of what the paragraph is about. Or it gives them one last idea to think about.

> Thanks to the snowstorm, we had a free afternoon! **(reminds readers about the subject)**

# Types of Paragraphs

There are four basic types of paragraphs: **narrative, descriptive, expository,** and **persuasive.** Each one does something different.

## Narrative Paragraph

A **narrative** paragraph by Caroline Starck tells a story about an event in her life. As you read the sample below, watch for details that make the story funny and real.

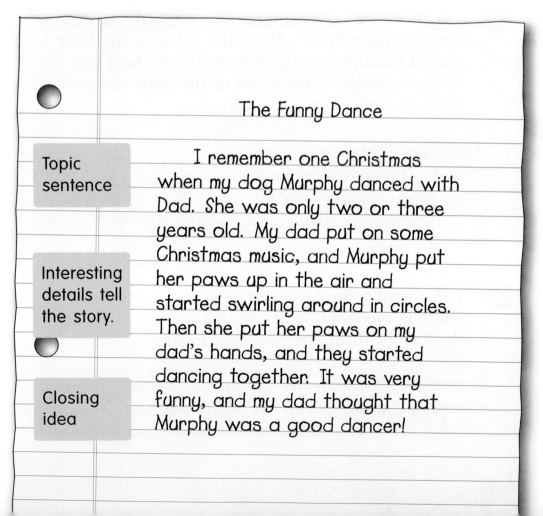

The Funny Dance

**Topic sentence**

I remember one Christmas when my dog Murphy danced with Dad. She was only two or three years old. My dad put on some Christmas music, and Murphy put her paws up in the air and

**Interesting details tell the story.**

started swirling around in circles. Then she put her paws on my dad's hands, and they started dancing together. It was very

**Closing idea**

funny, and my dad thought that Murphy was a good dancer!

## Descriptive Paragraph

A **descriptive** paragraph describes a person, place, or thing. A good descriptive paragraph uses words that help readers *see, hear, smell, feel,* and *taste* the subject. As you read the sample, watch for good descriptive words.

**Topic sentence**

**Details give smells, sights, and sounds.**

**Best detail saved for last**

### Zev's Deli

Zev's Deli is one of my favorite places to visit. When you walk in the door, you smell corned beef and fresh coffee and 100 other great smells. There are shelves everywhere, crammed with all kinds of food. There are bottles of olive oil, jars of pickles, and boxes and boxes of crackers. You can hear Zev yelling out people's names when their food is ready. My favorite thing to order is cheese blintzes. They taste soft and sweet and warm. Zev puts bright red strawberry sauce on my blintzes. Yum!

## Expository Paragraph

An **expository** paragraph explains something or gives information. It includes all the facts a reader needs to understand the subject. As you read the sample below, watch for words that explain.

 In some expository paragraphs, time words *(first, second, third)* are used to keep the main ideas in order.

### Living with a Little Brother

**Topic sentence**

Living with my little brother can be hard. First, he tries to copy me. If I have a second glass of milk, he does, too. Second, he

**Details explain the subject.**

always wants to play with my friends. If we play basketball, he wants to join in. But he is too small. Third, he wants to stay up as long as I do. He always says to my mom, "But Tim gets to stay up later." My mom says that he looks up to me, and I should be proud

**Closing idea**

about that. I'm trying to be, but it is not always easy.

## Persuasive Paragraph

A **persuasive** paragraph gives an opinion about something and tries to get readers to agree. As you read the sample below, watch for reasons that make the writer's opinion strong.

Topic sentence (states an opinion)

Details give reasons.

Closing sentence

**The Way to Go!**

Our neighborhood needs sidewalks. It is dangerous and hard to get around without them. We can't ride our bikes because our parents won't let us ride in the road. We can't use our in-line skates or skateboards either. In the winter, we can't even walk to our friends' houses because the snow piles up on the sides of the road. We are stuck playing in our own yards. Other neighborhoods have sidewalks, so we should, too.

# Writing a Paragraph

## Prewriting

**Select a Subject** ● Choose a subject that interests you.

**Collect Details** ● Gather your facts and examples.

- For a narrative paragraph, answer *What happened? Who was in the story? Where and when did it happen?*
- For a descriptive paragraph, collect *sights, sounds, smells, tastes,* and *textures.*
- For an expository paragraph, gather important *facts* and *examples.*
- For a persuasive paragraph, list *reasons* that support your opinion.

## Writing a Draft

### Put Your Information in Order

- Start with your topic sentence.
- Explain the subject in the middle sentences (the body).
- Sum everything up in the closing sentence.

## Revising

**Check Your First Draft** ● Look closely at each part—the topic sentence, the body, and the closing.

- Are your sentences clear and in the best order?
- Do you need to add more details about your subject? (Check the samples on pages 60-63 for help.)

## Editing & Proofreading

**Correct Your Writing** ● Use these questions as a guide when you check your revised writing for errors:

- Are your words interesting and colorful (*soft* or *sweet* instead of *good*)?
- Have you used the right words, and are your words spelled correctly?
- Does each of your sentences begin with a capital letter and end with the correct punctuation mark?
- Did you indent your paragraph?

# Writing a Summary

You learn a lot from reading chapters in books, articles in magazines, or documents on the Internet. Sometimes you must share the information in a special project or report. Writing a summary is a handy way to do this.

## Panning for Gold

A **summary** contains the most important ideas from your reading. You sift out the golden nuggets, or main ideas, and leave the rest behind. Then you combine your thoughts into a clear paragraph.

## Original Reading Selection

Read this article about the earth. Then study the summary below. The summary includes only main ideas.

### Our Earth: Sphere of Land and Water

Astronauts looking down at the earth from space see a **sphere** that looks like a beautiful globe. About one-fourth of the earth's surface is land. The rest, about three-fourths of the total surface, is water.

The largest bodies of water are the **oceans.** The oceans are not really separate bodies of water, but one great ocean. This great ocean is divided into four parts: the Pacific Ocean, the Atlantic Ocean, the Indian Ocean, and the Arctic Ocean.

The land on the surface of the earth is divided into **continents:** North America, South America, Europe, Asia, Australia, Antarctica, and Africa. The continents float in the one great ocean like islands.

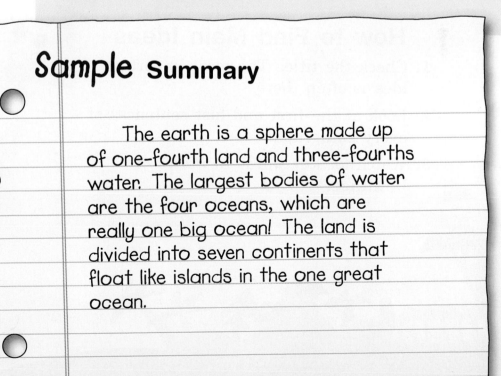

## Sample Summary

The earth is a sphere made up of one-fourth land and three-fourths water. The largest bodies of water are the four oceans, which are really one big ocean! The land is divided into seven continents that float like islands in the one great ocean.

# Writing a Summary

**Prewriting**

**Read Carefully** ● Learn as much as you can from the reading assignment.

- Read the assignment once to get the general meaning.
- Then read it again, more closely.
- Next, find the main ideas and list them on your paper. (See the steps below for help.)

## How to Find Main Ideas

1. Check the title. The most important idea is often there.

2. Look at the first and last sentences of every paragraph.

3. Watch for key words in *italics* or **boldface.**

## Writing a Draft

**Write Smooth Sentences** ● Use your own words, except for key words.

- Your first sentence should tell the most important idea.
- In the rest of your summary, include the other main ideas.

## Revising

**Read and Review** ● Ask the following questions:

- Do my sentences make sense?
- Have I included all the important ideas?
- Are the ideas in the best order?
- Have I put in too many details?

## Editing & Proofreading

**Check for Errors** ● Check your spelling, capitalization, and punctuation. Then write a neat final copy to share.

# Writing Sentences

# Writing Basic
# Sentences

Does "I broccoli" make sense? No, something is missing. Does "I like broccoli" sound any better? It should (even if you don't like broccoli). The second example states a complete thought.

## Making Sense

A group of words that states a complete thought is called a **sentence.** You use sentences when you talk to other people. You use sentences in your writing, and you read them in your favorite stories and books. In other words, you use sentences all the time. What do you need to know about sentences to use them well? Review the next two pages to find out. (Also see pages 322-325.)

*I like broccoli.*

*grow dislike eat*
*steam cook*
*chop*

# Sentence Parts

## Subject

All sentences have a subject and a verb. The **subject** names who or what is doing something.

**Su draws dinosaurs.**

## Verb (Predicate)

One type of **verb** tells the action of the sentence. It is called an action verb.

**Su draws dinosaurs.**

Another type of verb links the subject to another word in the sentence. It is called a linking verb.

**Dinosaurs are awesome.**

Remember, the subject and verb must go together. You must use a singular verb with a singular subject, and a plural verb with a plural subject. (See page 324.)

## Modifiers

In addition to a subject and a verb, most sentences contain **modifiers.** Modifiers describe or modify nouns or pronouns.

**Su draws giant dinosaurs on huge pieces of brown paper.**

# Sentence Problems

## Sentence Fragment

A fragment is a sentence that is missing one of its parts.

Gave her dog a bath. (A subject is missing.)

Corrected Sentence:

**Zina gave her dog a bath.**

## Run-On Sentence

A run-on sentence is two sentences that run together.

Mickey looked funny he was one big mess of bubbles. (This example is really two sentences.)

Corrected Sentences:

**Mickey looked funny.  He was one big mess of bubbles.**

## Rambling Sentence

A rambling sentence is one that goes on and on.

Mickey jumped out of the tub and he shook water over everything and then Zina got mad and ran after him. (Too many *and*'s are used.)

Corrected Sentences:

**Mickey jumped out of the tub.  He shook water over everything. Then Zina got mad and ran after him.**

# Combining
# Sentences

Sentence combining is making two or more short sentences into one long sentence. Here's an example:

Three Short Sentences:

> Heather likes slithery snakes.
> She likes skittery chameleons.
> She likes warty toads.

One Long Sentence:

> **Heather likes slithery snakes, skittery chameleons, and warty toads.**

## Why Combine?

**Combining sentences** helps you write longer sentences. A mixture of long and short sentences can make your writing more interesting and easier to read. You can learn how to combine sentences on the next page.

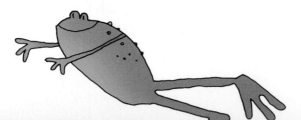

# Four Ways to Combine Sentences

## Use a Series

You can combine short sentences that tell different things about the same subject.

The desert is hot. The desert is sunny. The desert is dry.

**The desert is <u>hot</u>, <u>sunny</u>, and <u>dry</u>.**

## Use Compound Subjects

A compound subject is two or more subjects in one sentence.

Carlos speaks Spanish. Gaby speaks Spanish.

**<u>Carlos</u> and <u>Gaby</u> speak Spanish.**

## Use Compound Verbs

A compound verb (predicate) is two or more verbs in one sentence.

Gaby wrote a poem in Spanish. Gaby published a poem.

**Gaby <u>wrote</u> and <u>published</u> a poem in Spanish.**

## Use Key Words

You can move a key word from one sentence to another.
My mom flew to Japan. She flew yesterday.

**My mom flew to Japan <u>yesterday</u>.**

 Sometimes you can put a key word like "yesterday" at the beginning of your new sentence.

# Personal Writing

# Writing in
# Journals

Most authors write every day. Stories, magazine articles, movie scripts—they do it all. Most of them also keep special notebooks, or **journals,** for writing down interesting things they learn each day. Keeping a journal gives them ideas for their writing.

## Keeping a Journal

You can write in a journal as well as anybody else can (including your favorite authors). You have ideas pop into your head. You see things happen. You read and learn new things. Writing in a journal helps you think about everything you see and do.

# Writing in a Personal Journal

A **personal journal** is your own special place to write about anything and everything. You can . . .

- write about interesting things you see and hear,
- collect ideas for stories and poems,
- remember happy (and not so happy) times, and
- write personal letters and notes.

## Write about something you hear.

Tim's grandmother told him about going to school in England. Tim wanted to remember this story, so he wrote about it in his personal journal.

March 13

In Grandma's school, everyone had to learn to swim. They even tested her on swimming, and it was hard! She said England is an island, so the teachers wanted everyone to know how to swim. She also said that girls and boys had to play on different playgrounds. She only had one good dress for school!

# Writing in a Reading Journal

A **reading journal** is a place to write about the stories and books you read. Did you read an exciting or scary part? Is there something funny or something sad you want to remember? Is there a big word you want to write down? Do you have any questions about your reading? You can write about all these things and more in your journal.

Look at what Jamie, Doneen, and Lee wrote about. (Also see pages 274-275 for information about learning logs.)

## Sample Journal Pages

*Deserts* by Gail Gibbons
    The animals and plants in a desert look unusual to me. I'm very surprised that people live there, too. I hope I can visit a desert some time.
                                        —Jamie

*Sable* by Karen Hesse
    I wish I could have a sweet dog like Sable. I think it's good for a family to have a dog for a pet.
                                        —Doneen

*Author: A True Story* by Helen Lester
    This is a funny story (and serious, too) about an author who started writing when she was three years old! Ms. Lester, the author, made me think about being a writer.
                                        —Lee

# Making Albums

An **album** is a type of scrapbook—a place for special memories. An album may also be a place to collect things. Maybe you collect baseball cards, or stamps, or stickers. If you are interested in anything at all, albums are for you.

## Starting Your Album

Some students collect stamps in albums while others collect rare coins. You may even know of someone who has a vacation album. Here is another great idea: You can make an album about your pet or a special person.

# Making a Special Person or Pet Album

## Getting Started

Begin with a picture of your special person or pet. You can use a photograph, or you can draw your own picture. Then write something interesting or funny under it.

## Moving On

Here are some ideas to include in your album:

- Facts about your special person or pet (age, hair or fur color, eye color, size, and so on)
- When and how you met
- Things you like to do together
- Things your special person or pet loves or hates
- Strange or surprising facts about your subject

## Putting It Together

These tips will help you put your album together:

- **Make** a neat and colorful cover for your album.
- **Organize** all of your information so it follows a pattern. (You may want to organize the different pages in your album by first memories, middle memories, and last memories.)
- **Place** the pictures and words on each page so they are fun to look at and read.

# Writing Personal Narratives

On the way to school, do you ever say to a friend, "Guess what happened"? Of course you do. Everyone likes telling their stories. If you write your stories down, they are called *personal narratives*.

## From Telling to Writing

This chapter will show you how to write personal narratives so they sound just as exciting as the ones you tell. First read the student sample on the next page. Then begin your own story. (Follow the steps listed on pages 84-85.)

# Sample Personal Narrative

Here is a personal narrative written by Adam Kendall.

## Something's There

Last February, my dad and I were pulling down an old chicken coop in our backyard. I ripped off a board and saw something.

"What's that?" I said.

"It's just a pile of old gray rags," my dad said.

Then I yanked off another board, and I saw something pink and squishy-looking.

"Dad, can gray rags have a pink nose?"

Finally, Dad looked carefully into the chicken coop. "It's a possum! We just woke up a sleeping possum."

The possum walked away like it was dizzy. Then it disappeared into the woods. Dad laughed and I did, too.

# Writing a Personal Narrative

## Prewriting

**List Subject Ideas** ● Make a list of different things that have happened to you. Include happy, funny, strange, and important events.

**Select One Idea** ● Circle the idea from your list that interests you the most. If you can answer *yes* to the questions below, then you've selected a great idea to write about.

■ Do I have strong feelings (happy or sad) about this event?

■ Can I remember how things looked, sounded, and felt?

■ Would I like to share this story with others?

**Plan Your Writing** ● List the main things that happened in this event. (Or draw simple pictures of the main things that happened—like in a comic strip.)

## Writing a Draft

**Write with Feeling** ● Write your story as if you were telling it to a good friend. Make your story exciting!

■ Begin with words like these:
Let me tell you about . . . or
I'll always remember the time . . .

■ Use words that show how things looked and sounded:
I saw something pink and squishy-looking.

■ Use dialogue—the words people said:
"Dad, can gray rags have a pink nose?"

## Revising

**Read and Revise** ● Read your first draft out loud. Make sure you have included all of the important points and details. Also check to see that your ideas are clear and in the right order.

## Editing & Proofreading

**Check for Errors** ● Check each sentence for spelling and punctuation errors. Then write a neat final copy of your story to share with others.

# Writing Lists

Moms, dads, mayors, mechanics, coaches, cooks—all kinds of people write **lists.** Lists make jobs a little easier to complete. Take a look at the shopping list a zookeeper made to feed 10 animals. (These must be *mega*-animals!)

800 pounds alfalfa
30 pounds apples
25 loaves bread
30 pounds carrots
25 pounds potatoes
60 bananas
worms

## Making Lists

Lists can help you remember things, collect ideas for writing, think in different ways, or just have fun. Once you start listing, you won't want to stop.

### 1 Remembering Things

If you need to remember things at home or at school, just make a list. One student made a list of the things he needed for his science project.

### 2 Collecting Ideas for Writing

During one cold winter, students in Troy, New York, made a long list of winter words. They listened for winter words on radio and TV and looked for them in the newspaper. After two weeks, they had a list of 50 different ways to say or show, "It's cold!"

These students used their word list to write tall tales and personal stories about winter. List making gave them great writing ideas!

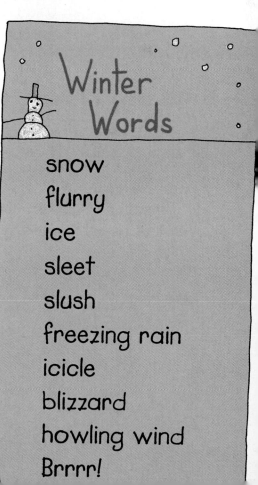

Winter Words

snow
flurry
ice
sleet
slush
freezing rain
icicle
blizzard
howling wind
Brrrr!

Science project:

glue
colored paper
tape
colored pencils
string
crayons
tissue scraps

### 3 Thinking in Different Ways

Lists can help you open your mind to new thoughts. There is a book for adults called *14,000 Things to Be Happy About.* The writer of this book thought about being happy in many different ways. Here are some of the things listed in the book:

- soccer socks
- when friends drop in
- toasting marshmallows
- (plus 13,997 more things to be happy about!)

**Students Try It Out** ● Students in Beaufort, South Carolina, made their own list of 100 things that make them happy. They wrote their list on a poster and hung it up in their classroom. Here are five of the things they listed:

## 1☺☺ HAPPY THINGS

We are happy about . . .
eating pancakes
riding a bike
staying overnight at a
    friend's house
fishing with Dad
baking with Grandma

## Having Fun

**A List Poem** ● A list can be a poem. Often the title says what the list is about.

### What Makes Me Laugh?

Silly songs and knock-knock jokes,
Snowflakes landing on my nose.
Kittens playing with a string,
Every creepy-crawly thing.
The knobby knees of a tall giraffe,
Hearing other people laugh!

**Silly Shopping List** ● To have fun, Yoshiko wrote a shopping list from A to Z for a hippo.

| | |
|---|---|
| A. apples | D. donut holes |
| B. bananas | E. eggplants |
| C. chocolate cakes | F. frosted cereal |

The list ends with *zucchinis*. Can you guess what comes in between *frosted cereal* and *zucchinis*? Try.

**Your Shopping List** ● Make your own shopping list. List 10, 20, 30, or however many items you need. Shop for yourself, your little brother, your favorite animal, or anyone else. Shop for yummy foods, yucky foods, or foods no one has heard of before. (Have fun!)

# Writing
# Friendly Notes

Has anyone ever given you a note? Maybe Mom or Dad left a note in your lunch box. Maybe your teacher wrote you a note about your report. Maybe your best friend sent you an e-mail message.

Christopher,
Don't forget to eat your carrots.
Mom BUGGING You

## Short and Quick

You can write **notes and e-mail messages** faster and easier than letters. Plus, you don't have to address an envelope or find a stamp! You can hand a note to someone, put it where the person will find it, or e-mail it. The fun starts when you get a note back!

# Great Reasons to Send Notes

You can send a friendly note at any time and for any reason. Think about the following four reasons:

## To Say Thank You

Has someone done something special for you? Is there someone you really should thank? Thank them in a note.

Dear Mr. Curtis,

Thanks so much for finding my snake. You are the best school custodian in the world!

Carlo

## To Ask a Favor

Sometime you may want to ask someone for a favor.

Dear Mrs. Williams,

I have a favor to ask you. (I hope you say yes!) May I sit near Shauna B. sometime this year? She's my new friend.

Thank you,
Brianna

## To Send a Special Message

Sometimes it's important to tell a friend that he or she is special. Remember, you can e-mail your messages, too.

Dear Luz,

Last weekend we went to a wildlife park. There were all kinds of colorful birds. I thought of you because I know you love birds. I wanted you to be there with me.

Love,
Maria

## To Give a Reminder

Notes and e-mail messages are often used to give someone a reminder.

Jakub,

Don't forget about Saturday. Everyone is going to meet at my house at 9:30. Then my dad will drive us to the game.

See you Saturday,
Chris

# Fun Note Ideas

1. Use special paper.

2. Decorate your note with a picture.

3. Add some special touch (a secret code, a riddle, and so on) to make your note interesting.

Susie,
   This star is for you. Can you guess why?
                Ms. Carey

Ari,
   Let's get together after school. Okay?

Teddy

Dear Blue Eyes,
   Open the clock's face. That's when we'll meet. See ya.

Lonestar

at 2:15 P.M.

Try writing a note to a new classmate or neighbor. You may start a new friendship that way.

# Writing
# Friendly Letters

It's fun to write a **friendly letter,** and even more fun to receive one. Letters keep you in touch with faraway friends and relatives. They can also put you in touch with someone you admire, like a sports hero or an author.

## Parts of a Friendly Letter

Friendly letters have five parts: the *heading,* the *salutation,* the *body,* the *closing,* and the *signature.*

1. The **heading** includes your address and the date.

2. The **salutation**, or greeting, usually begins with the word "Dear" and is followed by the name of the person you are writing to. Place a comma after the name.

3. The **body** of the letter contains your thoughts and ideas.

4. The **closing** can be anything from "Love" to "See you soon." Follow the closing with a comma.

5. Put your **signature** below your closing.

# Sample Friendly Letter

Andrea Curé wrote to Ms. Nathan, her teacher who had moved away. Ms. Nathan had sent Andrea a picture along with her letter.

**1** 1256 Cherry Street
Troy, MI 48003
March 2, 2001

**2** Dear Ms. Nathan,

You put hearts in the envelope!

You look great in the picture! Wow, traveling to Yosemite Park sounds cool. And it's nice you and Dr. Nathan are doing something special every weekend.

**3** That's great that you are playing the Mozart Concerto in C, even though you are playing an easy version. Yes! I am proud of you. I am in Level 3 in piano.

Morse School is really looking great. They are almost done remodeling. I wish you could see it. I think we'll get to move back in soon.

My new teacher is Ms. Porter. Many of the kids you had last year are in Ms. Porter's class.

Please write back and tell me more about California.

**4** Fondly,

**5** Andrea

P.S. We've had a lot of snow this year.

# Writing a Letter

## Prewriting

**Pick Someone to Write To** ● Maybe your best friend has moved away, and you miss her or him. Or maybe you would like to write to a favorite grown-up. Then there are all those famous people you admire.

**Plan What You Will Say** ● Make a short list of the things you want to say. Jamar's list for a letter to his friend Manny looked like this:

- new school year
- friends
- baseball results
- Manny's new home

## Writing a Draft

**Include Your Best Ideas** ● Pick one idea from your list to get you started. Then keep adding ideas and details until you say everything you want to say.

## Revising

**Review Your Work** ● Keep in mind, you won't be there to explain yourself when the person gets your letter. So make sure it is clear and complete.

- Do you need to explain anything better?
- Does your letter have interesting details?

## Editing & Proofreading

**Check for Errors** ● Review your letter for careless mistakes.

- Check for spelling and punctuation errors.
- Write a neat final copy to send.
- Make sure you have correctly addressed the envelope.

When you write to people you know very well, you can add personal touches like doodles or drawings.

# Writing
# Family Stories

Many families have stories they like to tell over and over. Kevin Lewis laughs every time someone tells the story about his uncle eating 17 pancakes. Jenna Bishop always asks her grandfather to tell the story about when he was 11 years old and drove his family from Maine to Arizona.

## Sharing Parts of Life

**Family stories** come in all shapes and sizes. Some stories can be told in a few lines. Others may go on and on. These stories show how families can be brave, funny, or strong. They're also fun to write!

# Sample Family Stories

### Pass the Pancakes

Once my uncle ate 17 pancakes! My father bet Uncle Pete he could eat more, but he got sick after 14. Later, my father said he should have skipped the syrup. My mother was mad. She said, "Grown men should know better!"

Every time we have pancakes, I think of my uncle. I think of my father, too. I use strawberry jam, but I can only eat four.

### On the Road

Would you believe an 11-year-old boy drove from Maine to Arizona? My grandfather did! His father had died and his mother wanted to move, but she didn't know how to drive. So her brother taught Grandpa, and he drove the whole way.

Grandpa said the worst part was listening to everybody complain. His sister kept crying, "It's not fair. I want a turn." His brother kept crying, "I'm going to be sick." His mother kept yelling, "Watch out!" It's amazing they made it all the way to Arizona.

# Writing a Family Story

## Prewriting

**Read and Remember** ● Think of family stories related to the ideas listed below. For example, Kevin would have remembered Uncle Pete eating pancakes after thinking about "food."

| | | | |
|---|---|---|---|
| animals | tricks | food | games |
| holidays | visits | trips | school days |

**Choose a Story** ● Choose your favorite family story to write about. List names and details to make sure that you remember the story. (Or ask a family member to retell it for you.)

## Writing a Draft

**Begin with an Exciting Idea** ● Kevin started his story with a surprising fact: "Once my uncle ate 17 pancakes!"

**Put in Details** ● In her story, Jenna added details to tell just what the trip was like. She included information about a crying sister, a sick brother, and a nervous mother.

## Revising

**Review Your First Draft** ● As you read, listen for things to change.

- Did you forget any important details?
- Are any of your sentences hard to read?
- Would one of your sentences sound better in a different place?

**Share Your Writing** ● Get together with a group of classmates and read your stories out loud. Listen carefully so you can tell each other what you like and what you wonder about. You may get some good ideas for making your story even better.

## Editing & Proofreading

**Check for Errors** ● Make sure all of your sentences are clear. Does each one begin with a capital letter and end with a period, an exclamation point, or a question mark? Also check for spelling errors. Then write a neat final copy of your story.

 Be sure to share your story with others.

# Subject Writing

# Writing
# Alphabet Books

Have you ever had fun with a jump-rope jingle?

**A** My name is **A**lice, and my brother's name is **A**l.
We come from **A**labama, and we sell **a**pples.

**B** My name is **B**radley, and my sister's name is **B**arb.
We come from **B**uffalo, and we sell **b**ananas.

When you put a funny jingle or other interesting information in ABC order in a journal or blank book, you are writing an **alphabet book.**

## Going From A to Z

There are alphabet books about every subject—**a**irplanes, **b**aseball, **c**ats, **d**ogs, **e**nergy, **f**ish, **g**eography, . . . See how easy it is? On the pages that follow, you can learn more about alphabet books and how to begin one of your own.

# Sample Alphabet Facts

Here are parts of two alphabet books. Carlos organized his book by finding a dinosaur for each letter. He gave three facts for each dinosaur: the meaning of its name, its size, and its eating habits.

## Dinosaur ABC's

**A**llosaurus means "different lizard." This dinosaur was 34 feet long and weighed 4 tons. It was a meat eater.

**B**rachiosaurus means "arm lizard." It was 85 feet long, weighed 70 tons, and ate plants.

**C**etiosaurus means "whale lizard." It was 45 feet long, weighed 10 tons, and was a plant eater.

Julie found 26 names of things in outer space—from A to Z. Then she found two facts to share about each thing. (This is the middle part of her alphabet book.)

### Outer Space ABC's

**L** The **Little Dipper** has seven stars and is shaped like a dipper. The North Star is part of the handle.

**M** The **Milky Way** galaxy has billions of stars. The earth and sun are part of the Milky Way galaxy.

**N** A **nebula** is a giant cloud of gas and dust. Stars and planets are born in a nebula.

# Writing an Alphabet Book

## Prewriting

**Choose a Subject** ● Think of a subject with lots of examples or parts, like *dinosaurs* or *airplanes*.

**List Related Topics** ● Make a list of topics, A to Z, about your subject. Carlos started writing the names of different dinosaurs in his list.

**Study Your Topics** ● Learn as much as you can about your topics. Write down notes as you read and learn.

## Writing a Draft

**Write the Facts** ● Give the same kind and number of facts for each topic. Carlos gave the meaning of each dinosaur name. He also told about each dinosaur's size and eating habits. Julie gave two important facts for each of her outer-space topics.

**State Your Ideas Clearly** ● Write interesting sentences for each topic.

## Revising

**Read and Review** ● Make sure that you have used the same kind of facts for each topic. Also make sure that all of your sentences are clear.

## Editing & Proofreading

**Check for Errors** ● Check the spelling of each of your topics. Also check your sentences for capital letters and punctuation marks.

**Plan Your Final Copy** ● Decide how the final copy of your book will look. Are you going to include pictures? Will your final copy be handwritten, or are you going to design your book on a computer? (See page 55 for bookmaking directions.)

"Alphabetical order" means to put words in the order of the alphabet.

# An Easy Alphabet Book

Here's how Jack planned his ABC book about flowers. You can make your book about a subject of your choice.

**First Step** Decide on a subject for your book. Then make three ABC lists. Here are Jack's three lists:

| People's Names | Action Words | Names of Flowers |
|---|---|---|
| Anna | admires | azaleas |
| Bart | buys | begonias |
| Chris | carries | clover |

**Next Step** Write a sentence using "A" words for the "A" page, "B" words for the "B" page, and so on. On each page, draw a picture to go with the sentence. Jack drew the flower to match.

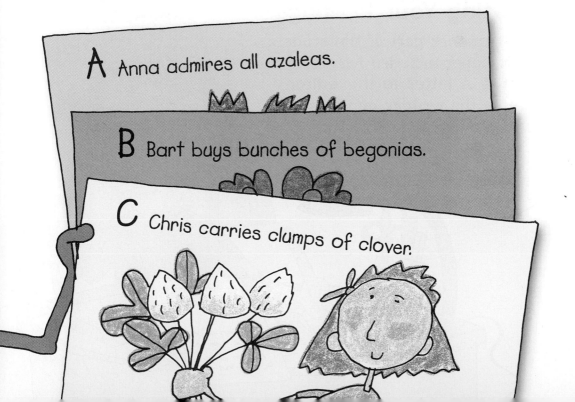

A Anna admires all azaleas.

B Bart buys bunches of begonias.

C Chris carries clumps of clover.

# Writing Newspaper Stories

Recently, one class started their own newspaper. It included news stories and human-interest stories. A **news story** reports on an important event. One example of a news story is a report on a recycling drive. A **human-interest story** reports on a topic that people will find interesting. One human-interest story told about students and their pets.

## Stating Your Feelings

Another part of the student newspaper included letters to the editor. A **letter to the editor** states the writer's opinions about an important topic.

# Sample News Story

## THE EXPRESS

**①** Room 202 Collects Cans

**②** *by Jesse Murino*

**③** The students in Ms. Grayson's class collected 22,000 aluminum cans in just six weeks. They asked parents to donate cans, and they found some themselves. The $1,200 from the can recycling will be used to buy trees for the south side of the school yard.

**④** "The children did a great job," said Patricia Gomez, the school principal.

"In years to come, people will look at the trees and remember these children."

Students felt bad when the budget for planting trees was cut. They tried to think of ways to raise money. Sam Jensen had the idea of collecting cans. Everyone thought it was a good idea.

**⑤** Ms. Grayson said, "I'm proud of these students for working hard to make the future better."

## Parts of a News Story

**1** The **headline** tells what the story is about.

**2** The **byline** shows who wrote the story.

**3** The **lead** tells the reader the most important facts.

**4** The **body** contains more information about the story.

**5** The **ending** gives the reader something to remember.

# Writing a News Story

## Prewriting

**Choose a Subject** ● Write about an important event in your school or community.

- Have you taken a field trip?
- Did your class just finish an important project?
- Is your community planning a new park?

**Collect Facts** ● Here are three ways to collect information for your news story:

### Interviewing
Ask different people questions about your subject.

### Observing
Study your subject very carefully and describe what you see and hear.

### Reading
Read about your subject to understand it better.

 News stories usually answer the 5 W's (*who? what? when? where?* and *why?*). Find answers to these questions when you collect information.

## Writing a Draft

**Write the Lead** ● The first sentence or two in the story is called the **lead.** The lead in your story should give important facts.

> The students in Ms. Grayson's class (who) collected 22,000 aluminum cans (what) in just six weeks (when).

**Write the Main Part** ● The main part of your story should state more facts and ideas about the subject.

> **More Facts** The $1,200 from the can recycling will be used to buy trees for the south side of the school yard.

**Write the Ending** ● Your ending should say something that helps readers remember the story.

> Ms. Grayson said, "I'm proud of these students for working hard to make the future better."

## Revising and Editing

**Check Your Work** ● Make sure you have answered the 5 W's in your story. Also make sure you have spelled all names correctly.

# Human-Interest Story

Some students in Ms. Angelo's class took a poll. They asked fourth graders what kinds of pets they had. Then the class wrote a human-interest story about their poll.

## Sample Human-Interest Story

### Dogs Win by Three

*by Room 204 Students*

**Begin with a catchy lead.**

For fourth graders in our school, cats are cool, but dogs rule.

**Include all the details.**

Ms. Angelo's class took a poll this week to find out what kind of pet was the most popular with fourth graders. More students had dogs than any other pet. Fifteen students had dogs. The next most popular pet was a cat. Twelve people had cats. Fish came in third with five people owning fish. Birds and hamsters tied for fourth place. Two people had hamsters and two people had birds. The most unusual pet was a snake. One student had a boa constrictor!

**End with an interesting idea.**

Dogs, cats, snakes—it really doesn't matter. Pets are a big hit with all of us.

# Letter to the Editor

One of your rights in a democracy is to give your opinions about important topics. You can practice this right by writing letters to the editor of your newspaper.

## Sample Letter to the Editor

October 12, 2000

Editor
The Express
Granger School
Charlotte, VT  05445

Dear Editor:

**Give your opinion.**

Third graders need the school library to stay open longer. In third grade, we are beginning to write reports, and we need to use the library after school.

**Give the main facts.**

Five parents have said they would work in the library after school. Many fourth graders would like the library to stay open longer, too. Fourth grader Gadi McBride said, "If the library stayed open, we could practice our computer skills."

**Ask for action.**

We hope you can discuss this at the next teachers' meeting.

Thank you,

Uri Levanon
Uri Levanon, Third Grade

# Writing Book Reviews

Everyone in Room 14 loves book-review time! Students who have written reviews love to share their ideas, and the other kids like hearing about new books.

## Sharing Your Feelings

In a **book review**, you can say exactly how you feel about a book. Is the book so good you wanted to stay up late to finish it? Did it make you laugh or think hard? Do you like the main character? Is there a lot of action? Do you think others would like this book?

# Writing a Book Review

## Prewriting

**Select a Book** ● Choose a book you are interested in. Choose an adventure story, a fantasy, a sports book—whatever you like.

**Collect Ideas** ● Use the questions on the next page to collect ideas for your review. Keep notes as you read.

## Writing a Draft

**Answer the Questions** ● Use your notes to help you answer the three book-review questions on the next page. Make sure to state the title and the author of your book.

## Revising and Editing

**Review Your Draft** ● Have you answered the three questions? Are your sentences clear?

**Check for Errors** ● Make sure you have spelled the author's name correctly. Also remember to underline or italicize the book's title. After you have checked your review for errors, write a neat final copy to share.

# Getting Started

Book reviews usually answer three questions:

1 **What is the book about?**

2 **Why do I like this book?**

3 **What main idea does the author share?**

## Sample Book Review—Nonfiction

Here's how Tamara Jones answered these questions in her review of a nonfiction (factual) book.

---

### Grow It Again

1 Grow It Again by Elizabeth Macleod is a book that tells you how to grow plants from fruits and vegetables. When you read this book, you will find out how to grow plants from things like beans, potatoes, peanuts, and kiwi seeds. It also has delicious recipes that kids can make.

2 I loved looking at the pictures and learning about so many different kinds of plants. I never knew about all those plants coming from the foods I eat.

3 This book tells how fruits and vegetables are good for you, and beautiful, too. You'll read about lots of food surprises.

# Sample Book Review—Fiction

Here's how Jake Maroni reviewed a fiction book. Each paragraph answers one of the review questions.

### Buster Makes the Grade

**1** <u>Buster Makes the Grade</u> is a book about Arthur's friend, Buster. The authors of this book are Marc Brown and Stephen Krensky. In this book, Buster is having lots of trouble with math, and he's afraid he might fail third grade. Arthur imagines that Buster will have to stay in third grade for thirty-three years!

**2** I thought this book was fun to read. Some parts made me laugh, but sometimes I felt sorry for Buster.

**3** The book shows you how you can change your mind about things you don't like to do. When Buster tries some new ways to study math, it works for him!

# Collection Chart

The questions in this chart will help you think about the books you read. There are separate ideas for fiction and nonfiction books.

## What is the book about?

Fiction: What happens to the main character? Where and when does the story take place?

Nonfiction: Is the book mostly about a person, a place, an animal, or something that happened?
Can you name one part of the book that seems very important?

## Why do you like this book?

Fiction: Does it have a lot of action?
Do you like the main character? Why?
Do you have a favorite part?

Nonfiction: Does the book contain interesting information?
Are the pictures helpful? Colorful?

## What main idea does the author share?

Fiction: What is the theme or message of this book?

Nonfiction: Why do you think the author wrote this book? What did you learn?

#  of Literature

The words listed below will help you understand and write reviews about stories and books.

An **autobiography** tells the true story of the writer's life.

A **biography** tells a true story about another person's life.

A **character** is a person (or animal) in a story.

**Dialogue** is the talking between characters in a story.

The **ending**, or resolution, brings a story to a close.

An **event** is a specific action in a story.

**Fiction** is an invented or made-up story.

The **moral** is the lesson in a fable, a tale, or another story.

A **myth** is a story created to explain a mystery of nature.

The **narrator** is the person or character who is telling the story.

**Nonfiction** is writing that is true.

The **plot** is the action in a story.

The **problem,** or conflict, in a story leads to all of the action.

The **setting** is the time and place of a story.

The **theme** is the main idea or message in the book.

# How-To Writing

**How-to** writing is everywhere—in science books, in cookbooks, in games, even on the back of cereal boxes. How-to writing usually gives directions. The directions explain how to do something. See if you can follow the set of directions below.

## Test Your FLEXIBILITY

1. First, stand up and put your feet together.

2. Next, bend slowly at the waist and try to touch the floor in front of your toes. Don't bend your knees . . . or bounce!

3. Then stay in this position for about five seconds. (If you can do this, you have good flexibility.)

# Writing Directions

## Prewriting

**Choose a Subject** ● Think of something you like to do, or make, or some special place you like to go.

**Select a Form** ● Decide if your directions will be in list form or in a paragraph. (See the samples on pages 123-125.)

## Writing a Draft

**Write Out the Steps** ● Either list and number all the steps in your directions, or write your directions in a paragraph.

**Choose the Best Words** ● Use words that make your explanation clear.

- Action words like *stand, put,* or *bend* tell the reader what to do.
- Time or order words like *first, next,* or *then* help the reader follow each step.

## Revising

**Read It Over** ● Carefully review your directions. Use these questions to help you review and revise your work.

- ■ Are my steps or sentences clear?
- ■ Are my steps in the right order?
- ■ Did I use exact words?
- ■ Can another person follow my directions?

## Editing & Proofreading

**Correct It** ● Check your revised writing for errors in spelling and punctuation. Double-check any numbers or measurements. Then write a neat final copy to share.

# Four Kinds of Directions

## 1 How to Make Something

Jenny explains how to make a butterfly hatchery. Study her action words—*punch*, *find*, *put*, *stand*, *replace*, *watch*, and *take*. These words tell the reader what to do.

## Making a Butterfly Hatchery

**Materials:** one large glass jar with lid, caterpillar, leaves, twig

1. **Punch** holes in the lid of a glass jar.
2. **Find** a caterpillar. (You might find one on a tomato plant, a tree, or a bush.)
3. **Put** the caterpillar in the jar. Also put leaves from the plant you found it on in the jar.
4. **Stand** a small twig up in the jar.
5. **Put** the lid on the jar. Put the jar in a shady place.
6. **Replace** the leaves in the jar every two days.
7. **Watch** every day. (First the caterpillar stops eating. Then it spins a cocoon on the twig. Finally, the cocoon splits open and a butterfly comes out.)
8. **Take** the lid off. Don't touch the butterfly. When its wings are ready, it will fly away.

For Rent

## 2  How to Do Something

The author of the following sample, Lamarr, explains how to recycle jars and cans. He uses words like *first*, *next*, and *finally* to let readers know the order in which to do things. This explanation is written in paragraph form.

### Recycling Jars and Cans

Recycling jars and cans is easy if you follow these steps. First, wash out all of your empties. Next, take the paper off them. Then put the clean jars and cans into a clear plastic bag or in a recycling container. Finally, put the recyclables out to be picked up.

## 3  How to Get Someplace

In this sample, Rachel explains how to get to her house from school. See how Rachel uses exact words for building names, street names, and addresses. She also uses the direction words *right* and *left*.

### How to Get to My House from School

1. After you walk out of the school's front door, turn left.
2. Walk two blocks. Turn right at the traffic light.
3. Walk three blocks to Moffitt's Market on the corner. Turn left. That's Hill Street.
4. Go down three houses. My house is on the right. My address is 3827 Hill. You should see our yellow door.

## 4 How to Have Some Fun

Writing crazy directions can be fun. Roberto's sample explains how to work his homework machine.

Roberto's Homework Machine

1. **Take** out the homework machine and turn it on.
2. **Whisper** in its ear exactly what it has to do. If you have three math problems, whisper, "You have three math problems."
3. **Put** your homework in your machine's mouth.
4. **Say** nice things to the machine while it works.
5. **Take** the homework out when the machine is done.
6. **Check** the machine's answers.
7. **Share** a treat if all of the answers are correct.
8. **Do** the problems yourself if the answers are wrong. (Have the treat by yourself, too.)

# Writing Business Letters

A **business letter** is not like a note or a letter you write to a friend. It is more serious, and it is usually about only one subject. Business letters look alike, too, because they always follow the same form.

## Taking Care of Business

Writing business letters can help you in many ways. You can send for things you want, ask for information you need for a project, or even try to solve a problem.

# Types of Business Letters

Two types of business letters are described on this page: *a letter asking for information* and *a letter to solve a problem.*

## A Letter Asking for Information

Let's say you need information for a science project. Or maybe you want to know how to join a fan club. You can write a letter of request asking for this information. Here's how:

- **Explain why you are writing.**
- **Ask any questions you have.**
- **State what you need.**
- **Say thank you for the information.**

## A Letter to Solve a Problem

Let's say you have to wait outside too long before the school doors open. Or let's say you ordered special dog treats for your dog, and the supplier sent you a book about dog tricks! You can write a letter to try to solve the problem. Here's how:

- **Describe the problem.**
- **Explain a possible cause of the problem.**
- **Suggest a way to solve the problem.**
- **Say thank you for any help you may get.**

# Parts of a Business Letter

Below are the six parts of a business letter. The sample letter on the next page shows each part.

**1** The **heading** includes your address and the date.

**2** The **inside address** is the name and address of the person or company you are writing to. If the person has a special title, add a comma and the title after his or her name.

Mr. Lee Cheng, Life Scientist

**3** The **salutation** is a way of saying hello. Use a colon (:) after the person's name. Use *Mr.* for men and *Ms.* for women.

Dear Mr. Cheng:

**4** The **body** is the main part of the letter. This is where you say what you want and give the important details.

**5** The **closing** is a way of saying good-bye. Use *Sincerely, Very truly,* or *Yours truly.* Always place a comma after the closing.

**6** Put your **signature** under the closing. If you are using a computer, skip four lines and type your full name. Then sign your name between the closing and your typed name.

# Sample Letter Asking for Information

Joey Jebrock sent a letter to a local expert, asking for information about the animal communities in the San Francisco Bay Area.

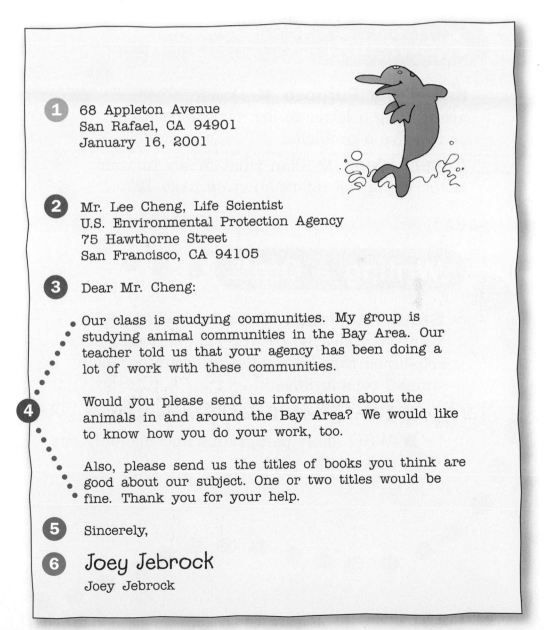

**1** 68 Appleton Avenue
San Rafael, CA 94901
January 16, 2001

**2** Mr. Lee Cheng, Life Scientist
U.S. Environmental Protection Agency
75 Hawthorne Street
San Francisco, CA 94105

**3** Dear Mr. Cheng:

**4** Our class is studying communities. My group is studying animal communities in the Bay Area. Our teacher told us that your agency has been doing a lot of work with these communities.

Would you please send us information about the animals in and around the Bay Area? We would like to know how you do your work, too.

Also, please send us the titles of books you think are good about our subject. One or two titles would be fine. Thank you for your help.

**5** Sincerely,

**6** *Joey Jebrock*
Joey Jebrock

# Writing a Business Letter

## Prewriting

**Know Your Purpose** ● Decide if you are writing a letter to ask for information or to solve a problem.

**Collect Ideas** ● Plan what to say in your letter, using the information on page 127.

## Writing a Draft

**State Your Ideas** ● Explain what you want very clearly. (In the sample letter, Joey explained that he wanted information about animal communities.)

- Follow the form for a business letter.
- Write short paragraphs and use only one side of the paper.

## Revising

**Review Your Ideas** ● Make sure you have included all the important information in your letter.

**Improve the Style** ● Make sure your letter is easy to read. Rewrite parts that don't sound right to you.

## Editing & Proofreading

**Check for Errors** ● Check your writing for punctuation and spelling errors. Make sure you have spelled all names correctly.

**Check the Form** ● Review the form of your letter. (It should look pretty much like the sample on page 129.) Then complete a neat copy of your letter to send.

T/P If you would prefer to send an e-mail message, see page 189 for information.

# Sample A Letter to Solve a Problem

The letter below is from a student who is trying to solve a problem.

1860 Ninth Avenue
Keystone, New York 12183-2031
October 10, 2001

Ms. Joan Putney, Superintendent
Keystone School District
623 Madison Avenue
Keystone, New York 12183-2048

Dear Ms. Putney:

**Describe the problem.**

I am in the third grade, and I am writing this letter to tell you about a problem. The kids on bus 26 get to school so early that we have to stand outside until the doors open.

**Explain the cause.**

Bus 26 picks me up at 7:30. The bus gets to school at 8:00. School doesn't start until 8:30, and the doors are locked until 8:20. It is cold in the morning. What will we do when it snows?

**Give a solution.**

I think we should be able to wait in the library or the gym. Some kids could read. Some kids could play ball.

Thank you. I sure hope you can solve this problem.

Sincerely,

Janna Morris

Janna Morris

# Sending Your Letter

## Addressing the Envelope

- Place your return address in the top-left corner of the envelope. Put the stamp in the top-right corner.

- The U.S. Postal Service suggests you use all capital letters and no punctuation marks when you address an envelope. Also use the two-letter abbreviations for states. (See page 311 for a list of abbreviations.)

```
JANNA MORRIS
1860 NINTH AVE
KEYSTONE NY 12183-2031



                    MS JOAN PUTNEY SUPERINTENDENT
                    KEYSTONE SCHOOL DISTRICT
                    623 MADISON AVE
                    KEYSTONE NY  12183-2048
```

## Folding Your Letter

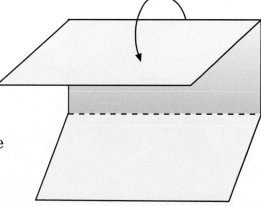

- Fold your letter into three equal parts.

- Crease the folds firmly.

- Put your letter into the envelope, and you're in business!

# Research Writing

# Writing Classroom Reports

The world is full of things to care about: dolphins, spiders, volcanoes, tornadoes, space, holidays, peanuts. (Yes, peanuts. Just think what life would be like without peanut butter!) In a report, you get to share all kinds of neat information about a subject that is important to you.

## Getting Started

Andy Levin liked and cared about hawks. He knew something about them from his dad. He found out even more when he wrote his report. This chapter will show you what he did to write a good classroom report. Then you can do the same.

Amazing Hawks
by Andy Levin

I have liked hawks for a long time
interesting thing about hawks is
If you knew what they ate,
that hawks aren't in ch
Hawks eat mice
A hawk kills a
claws ar
My

# Writing a Report

## Prewriting

**Choose a Good Subject** ● Choose a subject you care about.

- If you've been assigned a general subject like birds, make a list of your favorite ones.

- Look for more examples of your subject in an encyclopedia, in a book, or on the Internet. Also ask your friends or family members for ideas.

- Think about each example on your list. Choose the best one for your report.

**Write Questions About Your Subject** ● Think of questions that can't be answered with a *yes* or a *no*. Here's a good question: Why do hawks have such big wings?

**On Track** Copy your questions on note cards or sheets of paper. Put one question per note card. Or, you can copy your questions on a gathering grid. (See page 138 for a sample grid.)

**Learn About Your Subject** ● Use two or more different sources. Andy learned about hawks from an encyclopedia, a book, and his dad. Here is a list of sources you can use:

> **encyclopedias, books, magazines, newspapers, filmstrips, videos, CD's, the Internet,** and **interviews**.

**Answer Your Questions As You Read** ● Write your answers on the note cards or gathering grid. When you find important information, write down only the main ideas.

*If a book says . . .*

> Hawks capture small living animals as their primary source of food.

*You can write . . .*

What does a hawk eat?

It captures live animals for food.

# Gathering Grid

A gathering grid helps you organize the information you collect about your subject.

## Tips for a Gathering Grid

- Use a big piece of paper so you have space to write answers.
- Draw lines to form a grid.
- Neatly fill in the grid as you go along.

**Subject**    **Sources of Information**

| Hawks | Encyclopedia World Book | Book A Hawk's Life | Interview Dad |
|---|---|---|---|
| 1. What does a hawk eat? | mice, rats, snakes | live animals | snakes (tell story about Dad seeing one being eaten) |
| 2. Why do hawks have such big wings? | to help them dive at 200 miles per hour; some wing-spans 44"- 47" | to make them fly fast to catch prey | so they can fly high, and nest in cliffs |
| 3. About how long does a hawk live? | some live 30 years | | 10-15 years |

**Questions**

**Answers**

# Writing a Draft

**Write the Beginning** ● Your first paragraph should tell what your report is about and capture the readers' interest. Andy uses humor to hook his readers:

> If you knew what they ate, you would be glad that hawks aren't in charge of school lunches!

Here are other ways Andy could have begun his report.

■ Start with a question:

> Did you know that hawks can dive at 200 miles an hour?

■ Share an interesting story:

> My dad once saw a hawk eat a snake. . . .

**Write the Middle** ● Write the main part of your report. The answers to a specific question belong together in the same paragraph. For example, all of Andy's information about what hawks eat is in his second paragraph.

**Write the Ending** ● Make your ending strong. Tell what you have learned or how you feel about your subject. Andy wrote his last paragraph in this way:

> Hawks are amazing! They are as graceful as high divers and as fast as some airplanes. My dad is glad I've learned more about hawks. So am I.

## Revising

**Read and Review** ● The questions listed below will help you review your first draft. (Also have a friend or classmate review your work.)

■ Did you include a beginning, a middle, and an ending?

■ Is each middle paragraph about one idea? (Does it answer one main question?)

■ Are there any parts that sound unclear or that need more information?

## Editing & Proofreading

**Check for Errors** ● Check the spelling of all names and important terms. Make sure that all of your sentences begin with a capital letter and end with the correct punctuation mark.

**Plan Your Final Copy** ● Are you going to add pictures or charts to your report? Are you going to make a cover for it? Be sure to check with your teacher. You may be asked to write or design your final copy in a certain way.

# Sample **Classroom Report**

Amazing Hawks
by Andy Levin

**Beginning**

I have liked hawks for a long time. One very interesting thing about hawks is what they eat. If you knew what they ate, you would be glad that hawks aren't in charge of school lunches!

Hawks eat mice, snakes, and grasshoppers. A hawk kills a mouse by grabbing onto it with its claws and shaking it. Then the hawk pecks at it. My dad once saw a hawk eat a snake. He said, "The hawk chopped the snake in half and then gobbled up each half." Hawks eat grasshoppers whole. They need this food for energy.

Experts say hawks live a long time, but not longer than humans. Most live 10 to 15 years, but some live to be 30 years old.

**Middle**

Hawks have big wings and spend a lot of time flying. The <u>World Book</u> says that one kind of hawk has a wingspan of 44-47 inches. A hawk spreads its wings so it can get to its home in high cliffs. Another reason hawks have big wings is to help them dive at 200 miles per hour. This high speed helps them catch their prey.

**Ending**

Hawks are amazing! They are as graceful as high divers and as fast as some airplanes. My dad is glad I've learned more about hawks. So am I.

# Writing
# Photo Essays

Have you ever opened a book with photos and said, "Wow"? Many people feel that way. Photos in a book are very inviting. They can *show* you what words can only *tell* you. They make reading and learning more real and exciting.

## The "Show and Tell" of Writing

**Photo essays** share information or tell stories using words and photos. For example, in the book *Rosie, A Visiting Dog's Story,* by Stephanie Calmenson, the words tell how a dog cheers up sick children. The photos show Rosie at work in a hospital.

In this chapter, you'll see part of a photo essay by students just like you. You will also learn how to write your own photo essay.

# Sample Photo Essay

**Beginning**

Three students named Paul, James, and Shlomo created a photo essay about a resource teacher and her students. The title of their photo essay is "Helping Out: Mrs. Dulitz and Her Class." Here is the first page:

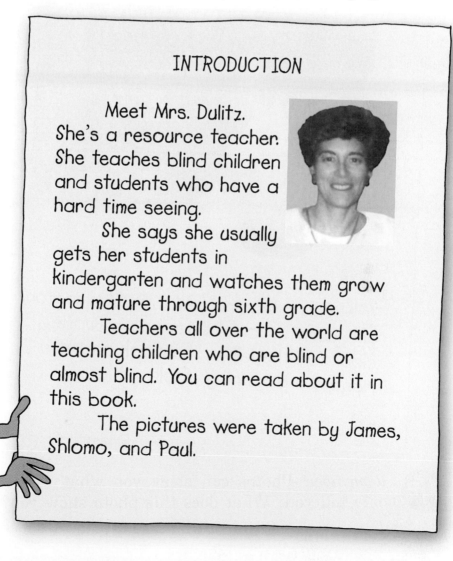

## INTRODUCTION

Meet Mrs. Dulitz. She's a resource teacher. She teaches blind children and students who have a hard time seeing.

She says she usually gets her students in kindergarten and watches them grow and mature through sixth grade.

Teachers all over the world are teaching children who are blind or almost blind. You can read about it in this book.

The pictures were taken by James, Shlomo, and Paul.

## Middle

The main part of the photo essay shows students using special equipment. Here are two pages from the middle part of the essay:

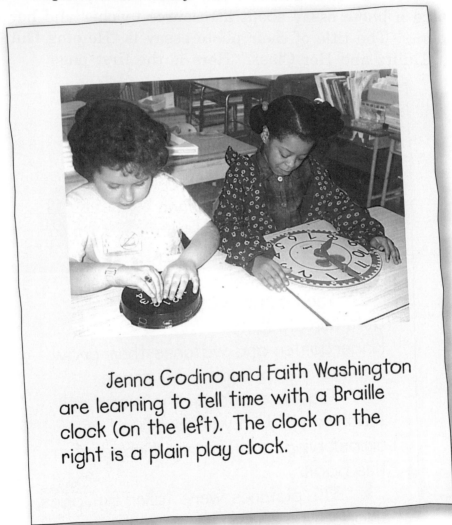

Jenna Godino and Faith Washington are learning to tell time with a Braille clock (on the left). The clock on the right is a plain play clock.

*Remember:* Photos can show you what words can only tell you. What does this photo show you?

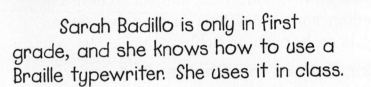

Sarah Badillo is only in first grade, and she knows how to use a Braille typewriter. She uses it in class.

### Ending

The photo essay ends with this look to the future. (There is no photo on the last page.)

Years ago there wasn't much technology to help the blind. Today we have Braille keyboards, laser canes, and talking computers.

Mrs. Dulitz and her class look forward to the future. Maybe there will be even better gadgets for her students to use.

# Writing a Photo Essay

## Prewriting

**Select a Subject** ● Make a list of different people with interesting jobs or hobbies. Choose one person for your photo essay.

**Learn About Your Subject** ● Write down what you know about your subject. Then ask this person some questions to find out more about his or her job or hobby.

**Take or Collect the Photos** ● Take or collect 10 to 12 photos of your subject doing different things. You could show a skater putting on her skates, practicing her skating routine, taking care of her skates, and so on.

**Decide How to Use the Photos** ● Think about which photos to use. Then put them in the best order for your essay.

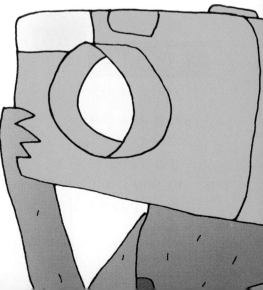

## Writing a Draft

**Tell Your Story** ● Write sentences to go along with your photos.

- Introduce your subject on the beginning page of your essay.
- End your essay with an interesting idea about your subject.

## Revising

**Read and Review** ● Look over your writing.

- Are all of your sentences clear?
- Do your words match with each picture?
- Did you include interesting details?

## Editing & Proofreading

**Check for Errors** ● Check your work for spelling and punctuation errors. Then make a neat final copy of your essay in book form. (See page 55 for help.)

# Writing Stories and Plays

# Writing Realistic Stories

Writers of **realistic stories** usually get their ideas from things that happened to them. They write about their experiences, but they change parts or add new details. The added material makes the real story into a fictional (made-up) story. Sometimes these stories are called realistic fiction.

As you read this chapter, notice how the sample story on page 150 sounds real. Everything in the story could have happened, but parts of it are made-up.

## Starting Out

A realistic story should sound like it could have really happened. You can even use a real event as a starting point. Just make enough changes so it becomes made-up. Read the sample and the guidelines on the next four pages to see how it is done. Then get started on your own story!

# Sample Realistic Story

Jonathan's story started with a real event, but a lot of his story is made-up. For example, he changed the names of the main characters, added some new details, and made the ending a little different.

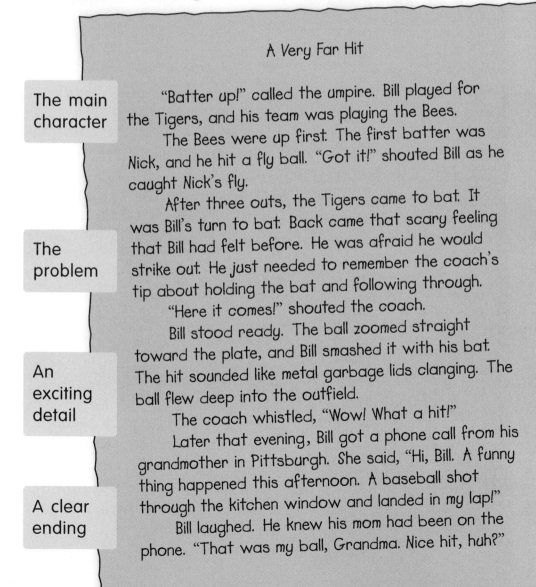

**A Very Far Hit**

The main character

"Batter up!" called the umpire. Bill played for the Tigers, and his team was playing the Bees.

The Bees were up first. The first batter was Nick, and he hit a fly ball. "Got it!" shouted Bill as he caught Nick's fly.

After three outs, the Tigers came to bat. It was Bill's turn to bat. Back came that scary feeling that Bill had felt before. He was afraid he would strike out. He just needed to remember the coach's tip about holding the bat and following through.

The problem

"Here it comes!" shouted the coach.

Bill stood ready. The ball zoomed straight toward the plate, and Bill smashed it with his bat. The hit sounded like metal garbage lids clanging. The ball flew deep into the outfield.

An exciting detail

The coach whistled, "Wow! What a hit!"

Later that evening, Bill got a phone call from his grandmother in Pittsburgh. She said, "Hi, Bill. A funny thing happened this afternoon. A baseball shot through the kitchen window and landed in my lap!"

A clear ending

Bill laughed. He knew his mom had been on the phone. "That was my ball, Grandma. Nice hit, huh?"

# Writing a Realistic Story

## Prewriting

**Choose a Topic** ● You may already have a good idea for a story. If not, follow these steps:

- List at least three exciting, funny, or odd events from your life.
- Select one of the events to use as the starting point for your story.

**Test the Event** ● If you can answer *yes* to these questions, your story idea is a winner!

- Can I remember a lot of details about this event?
- Will my classmates like to read about it?
- Can I think of ways to change it into a made-up story?

 **On Track** Your story should have a problem that needs to be solved. In the sample story, Bill was afraid he was going to strike out.

## Writing a Draft

**Choose a Way to Begin** ● You can start by writing down what really happened in the event. Or you can jump right into your made-up story.

**Make Things Up** ● Here are different ways to turn a real event into a made-up story.

- Change the names of the characters.
- Change where the action takes place.
- Change how the event begins or ends.
- Add more details to the story.

**Make Your Story Come Alive** ● Use action words and word pictures that make your story seem real. (See the next page for ideas.)

## Revising and Editing

**Read and Review** ● Read your story out loud. Change any parts that are hard to follow or that sound uninteresting.

**Check for Errors** ● Remember that your characters' words should be in quotation marks. ("Batter up!" called the umpire.) Also remember to start a new paragraph when someone new talks. After you check your story for errors, write a neat final copy to share.

# Making Your Story Come Alive

## Start Your Story with a Bang

Jonathan started his story in the middle of the action:

"Batter up!" called the umpire. Bill played on the Tigers, and his team was playing the Bees.

## Have Your Characters Think and Speak

Your story will seem more real if the characters think and speak.

Bill laughed. He knew his *mom* had been on the phone. "That was *my* ball, Grandma. Nice hit, huh?"

## Use Action Words

Action words help readers see and hear the story.

The ball <u>zoomed</u> straight toward the plate, and Bill <u>smashed</u> it with his bat.

## Make Word Pictures

Have some fun with your words to make your story exciting. A comparison that uses the word "like" or "as" can make an interesting word picture.

The hit sounded like metal garbage lids clanging.

# Writing Time-Travel
# Fantasies

Would you like to see a dinosaur up close? Or ride in a spaceship? Or meet King Arthur and the Knights of the Round Table? Well, you can . . . when you write a **time-travel fantasy!**

## Asking What If . . .

Fantasies often begin with a question:

- **What if** I found myself in a spaceship landing on a planet of robots?

- **What if** I crawled out of an old cardboard box and suddenly found myself nose to nose with a dinosaur?

- **What if** I suddenly appeared in King Arthur's court on my skateboard?

**TIP** To think like a fantasy writer, write a few wild questions of your own.

# Thinking About Time Travel

Before you begin a time-travel fantasy, you should think about an interesting time and place to write about. This page will help you make your travel plans.

**Choose a time.** Where would you go if you could travel into the past or future? Would you travel back to the days of the gold rush, or way back to the days of the dinosaurs? Would you travel into the future to a city on Mars? (See the time line on pages 382-391 for ideas.)

**Learn about it.** If you choose a long-ago time, read and learn about it. Start with an encyclopedia or the Internet. Jenna found these facts for her story, "The Dinosaur Club."

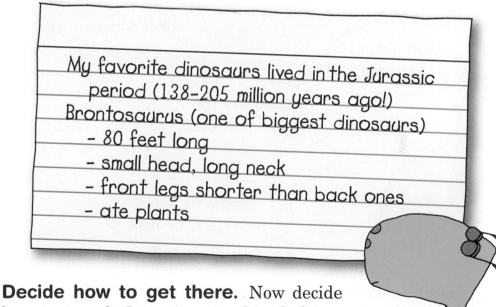

My favorite dinosaurs lived in the Jurassic
    period (138–205 million years ago!)
Brontosaurus (one of biggest dinosaurs)
    – 80 feet long
    – small head, long neck
    – front legs shorter than back ones
    – ate plants

**Decide how to get there.** Now decide how to travel. In a time machine? On a magical skateboard? In an old refrigerator box?

# Writing a Fantasy

**Prewriting**

**Invent the Characters** ● Pick one or two main characters to travel to the time and place you selected on the last page.

**Find a Problem** ● Choose a problem your characters face during their trip. Jenna made this cluster and then picked one problem for her story.

**Decide Where to Start** ● Make a list of possible places for your characters to begin their journey: the basement, the garage, the parking lot, . . . Choose one.

## Writing a Draft

**Take Off** ● Create your fantasy story.

- Have your characters do and say things that tell who they are.
- Show how and where they travel.
- Use the facts you collected.

**Include the Problem** ● Show how your characters get into trouble. Then, later, show how they get out of it.

In Jenna's story, a brontosaurus takes a radio that belongs to Maya's brother. Maya tickles the dinosaur under its nose until it sneezes and sends the radio flying.

## Revising

**Review Your Draft** ● Have you put in enough details to make your story interesting? Do your characters solve a problem? Make the changes you need.

## Editing & Proofreading

**Check for Errors** ● Look over your writing for spelling and punctuation errors. Then write a neat final copy to share.

# Sample Time-Travel Fantasy

Here's a time-travel fantasy by Jenna Thompkins.

### The Dinosaur Club

Maya walked into her backyard. She was carrying a portable radio she had borrowed from her brother's room. And she was dragging a big, empty refrigerator box.

"Cool!" said Maya's neighbor, Jonah, looking over the fence at the box. "We can make a fort!"

"It's going to be a clubhouse for my Dinosaur Club!" Maya said, thinking about the dinosaur book she had just read.

"What does the club do?"

"You'll see when you come inside," Maya replied, picking up the radio and crawling into the box. Jonah followed.

Suddenly the box began to spin and spin and spin. When it stopped, they tumbled out.

The main characters are introduced.

They travel in time.

**A problem occurs.**

An 80-foot-long brontosaurus walked toward them. Its two front legs were shorter than its two back legs, but they were still huge.

A loud song suddenly blasted from the radio. The brontosaurus picked up the radio in its teeth and then lay down and fell asleep.

**Excitement builds.**

"It's taking a nap!" Maya said with amazement.

"Let's go home!" Jonah whispered.

"No way!" said Maya. "If I don't get that radio back, I'll be in big trouble!"

Maya thought hard and came up with an idea. She picked up a branch that had fallen off a tree and tickled the brontosaurus under its nose. The brontosaurus sneezed and sent the radio flying through the air. Maya caught it and scrambled into the refrigerator box, pulling Jonah behind her.

**The problem is solved.**

The minute they were inside the box, it began to spin and spin and spin. When they peeked out, Maya and Jonah were home.

**The characters return.**

"Want to go again tomorrow?" Maya asked. "I'll ask my brother, too!"

"Okay!" said Jonah. "But let's not take his radio this time."

# Writing Plays

A **play** is a story that is acted out in front of an audience. People or animals in a play are called characters. They talk to each other and try to solve a problem. Plays can be fun to write because you get to tell the characters what to do and say.

## Finding Ideas for Plays

Ideas for plays are everywhere. You can write a play based on a real event or on a crazy idea you cook up. You can even write a play based on a well-known story. This chapter will help you turn a story into a play. On the next page, you can see what a play looks like.

# Sample Play

This is Scene 1 for a play based on "The Three Little Pigs."

## The Three Little Pigs

Cast

Characters: Pig 1, Pig 2, Pig 3, Wolf

SCENE 1

Setting

Setting: It is a beautiful spring day. The three pig brothers are in front of their houses. Pig 3 is putting the last bricks in a wall of his house. Pig 1 and Pig 2 are sitting in lawn chairs.

Stage directions

PIG 1: (with a laugh) Will you look at our goofy brother! He's still working on that brick mess of his. My beautiful straw house only took me a day to build.

Dialogue

PIG 2: Let's face it. He's always doing things the long, hard way. My wonderful stick house only took me two days to build.

PIG 3: (without sounding mad) Brothers, doing a job right is what counts, not how long it takes.

PIG 1: You're such a goody-goody.

PIG 3: Someday you'll thank me for building a strong house.

# Writing a Play

## Prewriting

**Choose a Story** ● List some of your favorite tales and fables. Look through a book of well-known stories to jog your memory. Then circle one of the stories in your list to turn into a play. Here's a list one student made:

> Favorite Tales and Fables
>
> "The Hare and the Tortoise"
>
> "The Lion and the Mouse"
>
> "The Three Little Pigs"
>
> "Cinderella"
>
> "Jack and the Beanstalk"

It may be fun (and a little easier) to write a play with a partner.

**List the Story Events** ● Write down the most important events in your story. Here's one example from "The Three Little Pigs."

Story Events
1. The three little pigs each build a house.
2. The wolf blows down the stick house.
3. He blows down the straw house.
4. Pigs 1 and 2 run to their brother's brick house.
5. The wolf tries to blow down the brick house.
6. The three little pigs catch him in a pot of hot water.

**Plan the Scenes** ● Divide the story events into scenes. A new scene means a new action is about to begin. (You can, however, include more than one story event in a scene.)

SCENE 1
The three little pigs each build a house.

SCENE 2
The wolf shows up hungry. He blows down the stick house. Then he blows down the straw house.

SCENE 3
Pigs 1 and 2 run to their brother's brick house. Pig 3 lets his brothers in.

SCENE 4
The wolf tries to blow down the brick house, but he can't. The pigs catch him in a big pot of hot water as he comes down the brick chimney.

## Writing a Draft

**Set the Stage** ● Write down the setting for Scene 1. The setting tells where and when the action takes place. (See the setting on page 161.)

**Write the Dialogue** ● Now write the scene by having your characters talk to one another. The dialogue has to tell the story. Your characters can talk any way you like.

    You can make your play funny by adding some modern words and ideas. You can also add stage directions to describe the characters' actions.

> WOLF: I'll huff, and I'll puff, and I'll blow your house down!
>
> PIG 3: (with hands on hips) No way, you big fur ball! These walls are superglued!

When you finish Scene 1, move on to the next scenes. Keep going until you finish your play.

## Revising

**Read and Review** ● Use these questions as a guide when you read and review your play.

- ■ Does each of your scenes deal with an important part of the story?
- ■ Do your characters' words and actions tell the whole story?
- ■ Is your play easy to follow?

**Share Your Script** ● Ask friends or family members to read your play out loud. Listen for words or ideas that you would like to change.

## Editing & Proofreading

**Check for Errors** ● Carefully check your play for spelling and punctuation errors. Then follow the form on page 161 and write a neat final copy of your play.

## Publishing

**Act It Out** ● The best way to share a play is to act it out. Actors must be selected and lines must be learned. Costumes and props are a nice touch, too. However, you may also share your play in a readers' theater performance. Characters read the script with lots of enthusiasm, but they don't need costumes or props.

# Writing Poems

# Writing Free-Verse Poetry

**Poetry** is . . . what poetry does. Poetry sings. It dances. It laughs. It cries. Poetry is rainbow words and star bursts and whispers. Poetry is the richest part of language.

What does all of that mean? Well, poetry is like life. It can be about good times, sad times, and in-between times. A good-time poem will be full of rainbow words and star bursts. A sad-time poem may be all whispers.

## The Poet in You

The good news is, everyone can write poems. This chapter will help *you* get started. You'll learn how to read and enjoy poems. And you'll learn how to write a free-verse poem. By the time you finish, you'll have all kinds of poems dancing in your head!

# Making Friends with a Poem

Once you start writing poems, you will probably enjoy reading them, too. When you read poems, you get to see how they look and hear how they sound. Follow these steps to make friends with each new poem you read.

- **Read the poem to yourself two or three times.**
- **Read it out loud.** (Listen to what it says.)
- **Share the poem with a friend.** (Talk about it.)
- **Copy the poem in a special notebook.**

Now make friends with this poem written by a student like you!

Elephant Poem

Rumbling
        Rumbling
Rumbling
12,000 pounds are coming.
Crashing,
bashing,
trashing,   mashing,
dashing,   gnashing,
on
        leaves.
Elephant noises all around.
                    —Claudia Mark

# What Makes Poems So Special?

## Poetry looks different.

It's not hard to spot a poem. It usually doesn't take up much space on the page. And it may have a very interesting shape, like this poem:

No Homework
When *my* teacher says,
"No homework"—
my heart
feels like the sky on the Fourth of July
firecrackers BANG!
s\*p\*a\*r\*k\*l\*e\*r\*s  sizzle
and
fireworks shoot high high high high
—Kevin Liu

## Poetry says things in special ways.

In Kevin's poem, he makes a special comparison: *"my heart feels like the sky on the Fourth of July."* He also uses descriptive words that make the poem come alive: *BANG, s\*p\*a\*r\*k\*l\*e\*r\*s,* and *sizzle.*

## Poetry sounds good.

Read Kevin's poem out loud. Listen for the rhyming words: *sky, July,* and *high.* Also listen for consonant sounds that are repeated: *feels, Fourth,* and *firecrackers; sparklers* and *sizzle.* Repeating sounds makes poetry fun to hear.

# Learning About Free Verse

There are many different kinds of poems. One kind is called **free-verse poetry.** A free-verse poem can be long or short. It can rhyme, but it doesn't have to. It can include special touches like s*p*a*r*k*l*e*r*s. You are *free* to write about your subject in your own way.

"Elephant Poem" and "No Homework" on the last two pages are good examples of free-verse poetry. Here is another one; it's a list poem.

When I Grow Up

When I grow up, I would like to BE
    an artist who draws cartoons of cats
    a gymnast who wins the gold
    a ballerina who twirls on her toes
    a seamstress who makes quilts and clothes
    a photographer who takes pictures
      of daisies and roses
    a teacher who teaches grade three
    a writer who writes books for kids like ME.

                    –Kristen Murphy

**On Track**

Kristen's poem looks a lot like a list. After the first line, she starts each new line in the same way: *"an artist who . . . ," "a gymnast who . . . ,"* and so on.

# Writing a List Poem

## Prewriting

**Choose a Subject** ● Use one of the subjects listed here, or think of an idea of your own:

- jobs I'd like when I grow up
- what I wish for
- things I've lost
- ways to be a good friend
- good news or bad news

**Collect Ideas** ● Write your subject in the middle of a piece of paper. Circle the subject and cluster ideas around it. (See page 264 for a sample cluster.)

## Writing a Draft

**List Your Ideas** ● Study your cluster. Then list your best ideas. Also add new ideas that come to mind. (If your poem is about jobs, start your list something like this: *When I grow up, I would like to BE . . .* )

## Revising

**Review Your First Draft** ● Use these questions to help you make changes in your poem.

- Do you like what your poem says? If not, rewrite some of your lines or add some new ideas.

- Do you like the way your poem looks? If not, think of another way to arrange your words.

- Do you like how your poem sounds? If not, maybe you need to add some rhyming words or words with repeating sounds.

## Editing & Proofreading

**Correct Your Revised Poem** ● Change or add punctuation marks and capital letters to make your poem clear. Check your spelling. Write a neat final copy.

# Making Pleasing Sounds

Here are different ways poets make their poems pleasing to hear:

**Rhyme** ● Using rhyme is one way to make pleasing sounds in a poem:

When I grow up, I would like to <u>BE</u>
a writer who writes books for kids like <u>ME</u>.

**Repeating Sounds** ● Repeating words can add special sound to a poem:

The wind came <u>tapping</u>, <u>tapping</u>, <u>tapping</u>
at my window.

Repeating consonant sounds helps, too:
<u>S</u>ail <u>w</u>ith the <u>w</u>ind on the <u>s</u>unny <u>s</u>ea.

# Making Comparisons

Here are some of the special ways poets make comparisons in their poems:

● A **simile** makes a comparison using *like* or *as:*
The race cars moved together
like a school of fish.

● A **metaphor** makes a comparison without using *like* or *as:*
Poetry is rainbow words and star bursts.

● **Personification** makes a thing seem like a person:
The shadow crept closer and closer.

# Traditional and Playful Poetry

The fruit section in a grocery store is full of wonderful choices. There are big red apples and small purple plums; plump green grapes and bright yellow bananas. There are little furry kiwifruit and giant striped watermelons. It's fun to try different fruits . . . even furry ones!

## Taste the Difference!

It's also fun to try different forms of poetry. This chapter talks about both **traditional** and **playful** forms. You'll learn about limericks and haiku poems, silly poems and shape poems. Fruit is good for you; it helps build strong bodies. Poetry is good for you, too; it helps build strong hearts and minds.

# TRADITIONAL Poetry

**Cinquain** ● A **cinquain** poem is five lines long. To write a cinquain poem, follow the form listed below.

One-word title . . . . . . . . **Sneakers**
Two describing words . . Bouncy, fast
Three action words . . . . Walking, running, jumping
Four feeling words . . . . Friends to my feet
One synonym for title . . Tennies

**Limerick** ● A **limerick** is also five lines long. Lines 1, 2, and 5 rhyme; and lines 3 and 4 rhyme. A limerick is always about a silly subject. Notice the rhythm of the words as you read it aloud.

> There once was a boy from Zion
> Who one day met up with a lion.
> He pulled on its mane
> And gave it a pain.
> But guess who ended up cryin'?

**Haiku** ● A **haiku** poem is three lines long. The first and third lines have five syllables. The second line has seven syllables. The subject of a haiku poem is usually something in nature.

> The butterfly lands
> on a bouquet of flowers
> tickling the petals.

# Writing a Haiku Poem

## Prewriting

**Collect Writing Ideas** ● Go outside and make a list of the things you see. You may see a blossoming tree, a busy insect, a sleeping cat, and so on.

**Select a Subject** ● Was there one sight you found really surprising or colorful or interesting? Select that idea for your poem.

## Writing a Draft

**Write Three Lines** ● Describe what you saw in the first two lines. In the third line, say something about your subject. Here's a first draft by student Kai Tan:

> The goldfish is shiny.
> He hides behind the weeds,
> Looking at the world.

## Revising

**Count the Syllables** ● Count the number of syllables in each line of your poem. Then add, take out, or move words to fit the haiku pattern:

Line 1: 5 syllables
Line 2: 7 syllables
Line 3: 5 syllables

**Check the Details** ● Make sure that you have used the best words to describe your subject. (In Kai's poem about her fish, she saw that "peeking" would be a better word than "looking.")

## Editing & Proofreading

**Check for Errors** ● Correct any spelling, capitalization, or punctuation errors. Then make a neat final copy of your poem. Here is Kai's finished poem:

The shiny goldfish
hides behind green wiggly weeds
peeking at the world.

# PLAYFUL Poetry

**Alphabet Poem** ● An **alphabet** poem uses part of the alphabet to create a funny list poem.

**C**arefree
**D**olphins
**E**ven
**F**lip
**G**racefully

**Concrete Poem** ● A **concrete** poem has a special shape or design.

Dizzy leaves slowly fall to the ground.

**5-W's Poem** ● A **5-W's** poem is five lines long. Each line answers one of the 5 W's (*who? what? where? when?* and *why?*).

My dog
curls up
on my bed
every night
because I let him.

# Writing a 5-W's Poem

## Prewriting

**Select a "Who"** ● Make a list of silly and serious "who" ideas. Select one for your subject.

**Make a 5-W's Chart** ● Use a chart like this one to list ideas for your poem.

| who? | what? | when? | where? | why? |
|------|-------|-------|--------|------|
|      |       |       |        |      |

## Writing a Draft

**Write Your Poem** ● Use the words in your chart to write your first draft. Use a separate line for each answer to a 5-W's question.

## Revising and Editing

**Check the Facts** ● Make sure that you have answered all of the 5 W's.

**Check Your Words** ● Make sure that you have used the best words in your poem. For example, "My dog curls up" is better than "My dog sleeps."

**Check for Errors** ● Correct any mistakes and make a neat final copy.

# Finding Information

# Using the Library

The **library** is a one-stop information place. It is loaded with facts, photos, and ideas on all sorts of topics. All of this information is found in magazines, books, newspapers, videos, CD's, and on the Internet. Libraries are sometimes called media centers because they contain so many different types of materials.

## Finding Your Way

Libraries are really helpful when you are working on reports and other big projects. This chapter explains how libraries are organized, and how you can find the information you need.

# Using the Card Catalog

You can learn about foxes by visiting the zoo. You can also learn about foxes by reading a book from the library. You'll need to use the **card catalog** to get started. It tells you which books are in your library. Each book usually has three cards in the card catalog.

 **Title Card:** There is a **title card** for every book in the library. If a title begins with *A, An,* or *The,* look up the next word in the title.

*Foxes for Kids*

 **Author Card:** There is also an **author card** for every book. The last name of the author comes first on this card.

Schuler, Judy

 **Subject Card:** There is a **subject card** for most books.

Look under the subject heading FOXES to find books about foxes.

# Tips to Follow

- If you know the title of a book, look in the card catalog (or computer catalog) for the *title card*.
- If you know only the author's name, look up the *author card*.
- If you know only the subject that you need information about, look up the *subject card*.

# Sample Catalog Cards

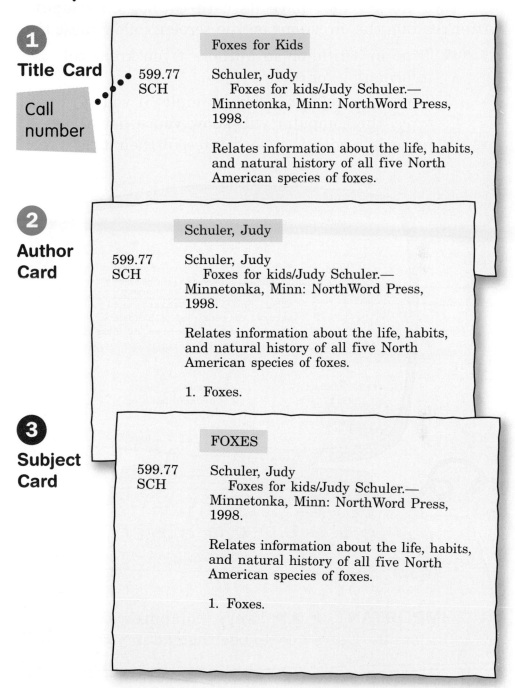

**1**

**Title Card**

Call number

> Foxes for Kids
>
> 599.77
> SCH
>
> Schuler, Judy
>     Foxes for kids/Judy Schuler.—
> Minnetonka, Minn: NorthWord Press,
> 1998.
>
> Relates information about the life, habits,
> and natural history of all five North
> American species of foxes.

**2**

**Author Card**

> Schuler, Judy
>
> 599.77
> SCH
>
> Schuler, Judy
>     Foxes for kids/Judy Schuler.—
> Minnetonka, Minn: NorthWord Press,
> 1998.
>
> Relates information about the life, habits,
> and natural history of all five North
> American species of foxes.
>
> 1. Foxes.

**3**

**Subject Card**

> FOXES
>
> 599.77
> SCH
>
> Schuler, Judy
>     Foxes for kids/Judy Schuler.—
> Minnetonka, Minn: NorthWord Press,
> 1998.
>
> Relates information about the life, habits,
> and natural history of all five North
> American species of foxes.
>
> 1. Foxes.

# Using a Computer Catalog

Your library may have its card catalog on computer. After reading the directions on the screen, follow these tips:

- ■ Type in a title or an author, if you know this information, or

- ■ Type in a keyword. For example, if you type *foxes,* the computer will show you a list of materials with the word *foxes* in their titles.

```
     Author: Schuler, Judy

      Title: Foxes for Kids

  Published: Minnetonka, Minn.: NorthWord
             Press, 1998 44 p.: col. ill.
      Notes: This book relates information
             about the life, habits, and
             natural history of all five
             North American species of foxes.
Added entry: McGee, John F., ill.

    Subject: Foxes

Call number:              Status:
   599.77 SCH             Checked out

   Location: Children's
```

**IMPORTANT** ▶▶▶ Every computer catalog is different. Learn how to use the one in your library.

# Finding a Book

Once you've found the card for a book, copy down the **call number.** The call number helps you find a book on the shelves.

## Finding Nonfiction

Nonfiction (factual) books are arranged on the shelves in number order. Here are some things you need to know:

- Some call numbers have one or more letters at the end. The book with the call number **973A** comes before **973B** on the shelf.

- Some call numbers have decimals, like **973.19** or **973.2.** They may be a little harder to find. Ask the librarian for help if you need it.

## Finding Fiction

Fiction books are arranged together on special shelves.

- Fiction books are in ABC order by the author's last name.

- Some fiction books have the first two letters of the author's last name on the spine, like **CL** for Beverly Cleary.

## Finding Biographies

Biographies have their own shelves, too.

- Biographies are arranged by the call number **921** and the first letters of the subject's last name. A biography about Abe Lincoln would be **921 LIN.**

# Using an Encyclopedia

An **encyclopedia** is a set of books (or a CD or Web site) that has articles on every topic you can imagine. The topics are in ABC order, just like words in a dictionary. Each article gives you a lot of helpful information. You may also find a list of related topics at the end of an article. If you look up these topics, you will find even more information about your topic.

Turn to page 191 to find out more about on-line encyclopedias.

# Using Other Reference Books

**Reference books** give a lot of useful information. Dictionaries and atlases are reference books. They are kept in a special section of the library. Here are some other common reference books that your library may have:

*Scholastic Kid's Almanac for the 21st Century* is an A to Z collection of information on nearly 40 topics.

*Heinemann First Encyclopedia* is a 10-volume encyclopedia covering animals, plants, countries, transportation, science, ancient civilizations, and world history.

*Something About the Author* tells about writers and illustrators and gives their addresses.

*From Sea to Shining Sea* covers the 50 states, the District of Columbia, and Puerto Rico.

# Understanding the Parts of a Book

Books are easier to use when you understand their parts. All books have some of the following parts:

- The **title page** is usually the first page with printing on it. It gives the title of the book, the author's name, the publisher's name, and the city where the book was published.

- The **copyright page** comes next. It gives the year the book was published. This can be important. An old book may have information that is no longer correct.

- The **table of contents** tells the names and page numbers of the chapters and sections in the book.

- The **chapter** and **section headings** tell what type of information is covered in each part of a book.

- The **captions** give important information about photographs, illustrations, or graphics. They are located near the pictures.

- The **glossary** explains special words used in the book. It's like a mini-dictionary. Usually the glossary is near the back of a book.

- The **index** is an ABC list of all the topics in the book. It also gives the page number where each topic is covered. The index is at the very back of the book.

# Using the Internet

The Internet connects you and your computer to other people and computers around the world. It lets you do some pretty amazing things! The Net (that's short for "Internet") is an electronic post office. It sends your e-mail (electronic mail) all over the globe. It helps you talk to authors, teachers, relatives, and friends—as though you were in a big clubhouse together. The Internet is also the world's biggest library, full of information, pictures, and sounds for you to explore!

# Using E-Mail

An e-mail message is like a friendly note or letter. You can attach pictures, sound recordings, and documents, too.

**1** **Send button** (Click here to mail your finished letter.)

**2** **Your e-mail address** (The computer puts this here.)

**3** **Receiver's e-mail address** (You type this in.)

**4** **Subject line** (You type what your message is about.)

**5** **Attachment** (Pictures, sounds, and text files can be sent with e-mail.)

**6** **Message** (Type your message here.)

# Viewing Web Pages

The Web is one part of the Internet. It is made up of "pages." Each page has its own electronic address. When you click a Web link or type a Web address, it moves you to another page. (Try it with **<thewritesource.com>**.)

## Parts of a Web Page

**1** The **arrows** take you back to the last page you visited (*left arrow*) or forward to the next page (*right arrow*).

**2** The **"home"** button takes you to your starting page.

**3** The **"print"** button prints the page you are on.

**4** The **address** line shows the address of the page you see. This is also where you type a new address.

**5** **Links** (colored, underlined words) will take you to other pages.

# Surfing the Web

Do you ever "channel surf" on your TV? Some people also surf the Web, moving from link to link, because there are so many interesting sites to visit. Here are a few examples of the types of sites you can find.

## On-Line Encyclopedias

If you want to look up something in a hurry, an on-line encyclopedia may be just what you need.

**Encyclopedia.com** <www.encyclopedia.com> This site offers many short articles on topics from A to Z.

**Britannica.com** <www.britannica.com> This site offers more-detailed articles.

**Letsfindout.com** <www.letsfindout.com>This site offers articles designed just for kids.

## Electronic Libraries

When an encyclopedia isn't enough, you may want to visit an on-line library.

**Internet Public Library** <www.ipl.org> This very useful library has many on-line magazines and newspapers and a special section just for kids.

**Library of Congress** <www.loc.gov> This is the United States Congress's own library. It's so huge, you may need help from an adult to find what you're looking for.

## Search Engines

A search engine is a special Web tool that helps you find what you need on the Web. To learn how to use a search engine, see the next page.

# Using a Search Engine

A search engine is a special Web site that lists addresses and descriptions of millions of Web pages. It has a computer program to let you search those pages.

## Parts of a Search Engine

**1** **Search box** (Enter keywords and then click on "Search.")

**2** **Index headings** (Click on a category to see what it contains.)

**3** **Help link** (Click this graphic for instructions.)

**4** **Featured links** (Each of these graphics and underlined words is a link to another page.)

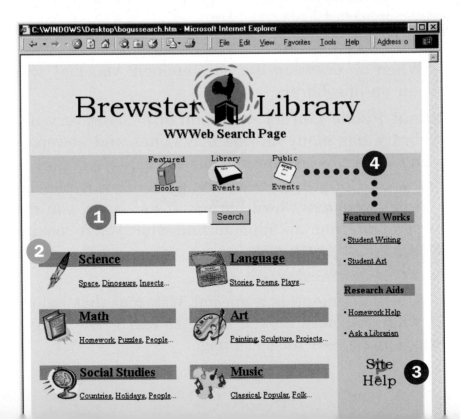

# Exploring the Net

The Net is a big, busy world, so you need to be on your best behavior as you explore it. Here are a few important guidelines.

### Ask permission.

Always ask an adult for permission before you go on-line, and especially before you send e-mail.

### Don't shout.

Using capital letters means you are SHOUTING. Shouting is hard to read and is considered impolite.

### Be polite.

Be both clear and pleasant in your on-line messages. Add a smiley to some of your messages. A smiley looks like this: :-)

### Be careful.

Never give your full name, address, or phone number on the Net unless your parents give you permission. Also, if you find a page that makes you uncomfortable, use the back button (left arrow) on your browser to leave it.

### Have fun!

Remember that the Net can be a great place to learn about your world. Enjoy it!

# Reading Skills

# Reading Graphics

You find **graphics** in many different places. They are on signs in your community, in directions about how to make things, and in the books and magazines you read. It is very important that you know how to "read" graphics because they help you learn.

## Look at This!

This chapter tells you how to read four different kinds of graphics: symbols, diagrams, graphs, and tables. As you learn about these graphics, you'll be surprised at how much information they can give. *Remember:* Understanding graphics is like reading . . . without all the words.

# Learning About Symbols

A **symbol** is a simple graphic, or drawing, that stands for something. Symbols can be divided into two groups.

**1. Some symbols stand for ideas or feelings.**

a.  b.  c.

**2. Some symbols give information.**

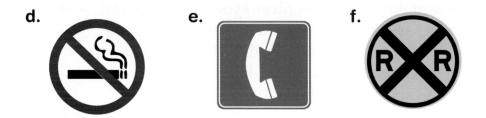

d.  e.  f.

# Tips for Understanding Symbols

■ **Look at the graphic and think.**
■ **Decide what it means.**

Figure out what each symbol on this page means. (Check your answers below.)

**a. Happiness, b. Love, c. Power, d. No Smoking, e. Telephone, f. Railroad Crossing**

# Learning About Diagrams

A **diagram** is a graphic that shows how something works or how something happens. When you read a diagram, be sure to check the labels and notice the direction of any arrows.

## How You Get Electricity

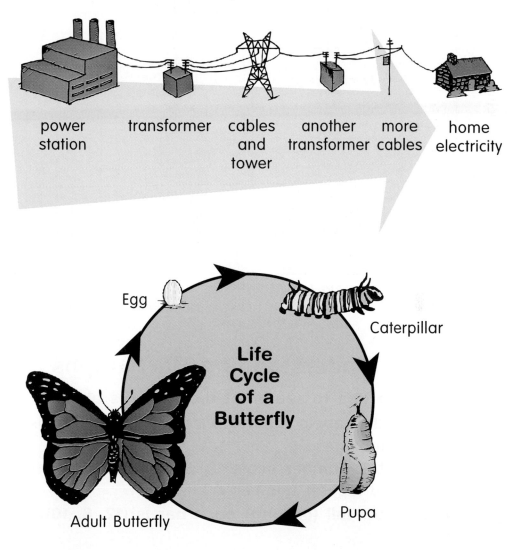

power station     transformer     cables and tower     another transformer     more cables     home electricity

Egg

Caterpillar

**Life Cycle of a Butterfly**

Pupa

Adult Butterfly

# Learning About Bar Graphs

A **bar graph** shows how two or more things compare. The bars can go up and down or sideways. Both bar graphs below show the same thing. Of the 28 students, 12 prefer playground equipment, 10 like kick ball, and 6 choose tag as their favorite recess activity.

**Favorite Recess Activities**

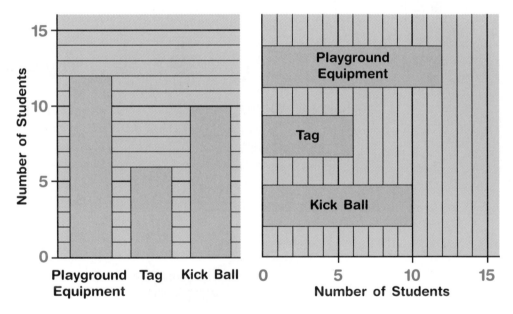

# Tips for Understanding Bar Graphs

- **Read the title to see what the graph is about.**
- **Look at the labels for the bars.** They tell what is being counted.
- **Look at the number scale (0, 5, 10, 15).** Notice the lowest and highest numbers.
- **Notice how tall (or long) each bar is (12, 6, 10).**

# Learning About Tables

A **table** is a graphic that has two basic parts: *rows* go across, and *columns* go down. Here are two examples:

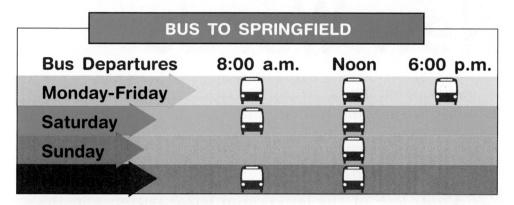

**BUS TO SPRINGFIELD**

| Bus Departures | 8:00 a.m. | Noon | 6:00 p.m. |
|---|---|---|---|
| Monday-Friday | 🚌 | 🚌 | 🚌 |
| Saturday | 🚌 | 🚌 | |
| Sunday | | 🚌 | |
| Holidays | 🚌 | 🚌 | |

### Classmates and Pets

| Kind of Pet | Girls Owning Pets | Boys Owning Pets | Total |
|---|---|---|---|
| Dog | 9 | 6 | 15 |
| Cat | 4 | 8 | 12 |
| Fish | 4 | 1 | 5 |
| Bird | 0 | 2 | 2 |
| Snake | 1 | 0 | 1 |
| Total Pets | 18 | 17 | 35 |

# Tips for Understanding Tables

- Read the title to see what the table is about.
- Look at the column headings.
- Read each row across.
- **Ask questions.** How many buses are leaving on Thanksgiving Day? How many students have cats?

# Reading
# New Words

When you see a word you can't read, use the following **reading strategies** to help you.

## Read and Check

First, look at the letters and letter patterns in the word you can't read. Next, say the sound each letter or letter pattern makes. Then blend the sounds into a word you know. The following tips can help you.

- Look for **consonant blends,** such as "str" in *string.* Say the blend and then add the remaining sounds of the word.
- Use what you know about **vowel pairs,** such as "ai" in *paid* and *rain.*
- Watch for **r-controlled vowels,** such as "ir" in *first* or "air" in *pair.*

Check to make sure the word you have said makes sense. If it doesn't, think about the other words in the sentence and try again.

## Look for Word Parts You Know

Longer words often have little words or word parts in them. For example, if you can read the little word *end*, you can probably read the words *bend, mend, send, blend,* and *ending*.

If you can read the word part *ight*, you can probably read the words *night, sight,* and *delight*.

## Look for Syllables

vowel/consonant, vowel—as in su/per

vowel, consonant/vowel—as in sev/en

vowel, consonant/consonant, vowel—as in sup/per

## Look for Prefixes, Suffixes, and Roots

Longer words may be made up of smaller parts that you know.

|  | | Prefix | | Root | Suffix |
|---|---|---|---|---|---|
| monorail | = | mono | + | rail | |
| lioness | = | | | lion | + ess |
| unhealthy | = | un | + | health | + y |

 Your handbook includes the meanings of many prefixes, suffixes, and roots. (See pages 216-225.)

## Look for Compound Words

Many big words are made up of two smaller words. We call these compound words. Here are a few examples: *sidewalk, farmyard,* and *basketball*.

# Reading to Understand

Being a good reader means understanding what you read. And understanding is what reading is all about. It makes reading enjoyable and meaningful. It helps you learn, remember, and discover wonderful things about your world.

## Ways to Improve Your Reading

- **Read often.**
- **Read a lot of different things.**
  (Read information books, newspapers, magazines, and Web sites.)
- **Read at different speeds.**
  (For example, slow down when there are a lot of facts in the reading.)
- **Use reading strategies to help you understand what you read.**
  (This chapter will show you how.)

# Reading Information Books

A **reading strategy** is a plan to help you with your reading. You can use the **think-and-read** strategy below when you are reading chapters in information books.

## Think and Read

### Before Reading

**Preview** ● Study the title, the headings, and the graphics.

**Think** ● Decide what you already know about the topic. Then predict what the chapter will say.

**Set a Purpose** ● Decide what you want to find out. Write down the questions you have.

### During Reading

**Pause** ● Think about each new idea as you read.

**Find Answers** ● Look for answers to your questions.

**Take Notes** ● Write down interesting facts.

### After Reading

**Review** ● Did the reading answer your main questions? What new things did you learn?

**Share** ● Talk about your reading with a classmate or a parent. Write about it in your journal.

## Know Want Learn

**KWL** is another good reading strategy. To use this strategy, you will need to make a chart. Here's how a completed KWL chart looks.

### Sample KWL Chart

Building Machines and What They Do

| K<br>What do I know? | W<br>What do I want to learn? | L<br>What did I learn? |
|---|---|---|
| 1. Building machines dig holes.<br>2. Some lift materials very high up.<br>3. Some stir cement. | 1. What are the names of all the machines?<br>2. What are some new machines?<br>3. How is a building made? | 1. About towers, cement mixers, crushers, excavators<br>2. There are lots of pipes underground when a building is made. |

**On Track** Look at your columns after you finish reading to see if you have answered your questions. Maybe you'll want to add a few more questions to the **W** column, and then read more about the topic.

# Mapping

**Mapping** is a reading strategy that helps you organize ideas about a subject. Begin by writing the subject in the middle of your paper. Then, as you read, draw a map of the *main ideas* and *details* about the subject. Here's a reading map for a book about sharks.

## Sample Reading Map

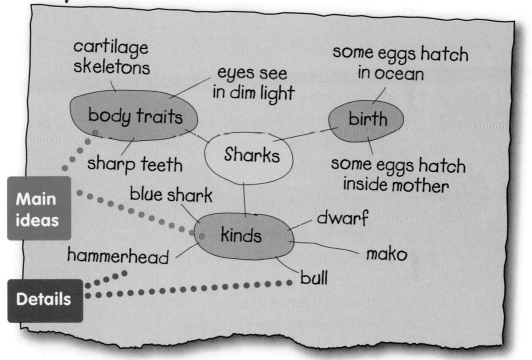

**Finding Main Ideas** ● When you read, look for main ideas. You can find main ideas in headings, in bold print, or in the first and last sentences of paragraphs.

**Finding Details** ● *Details* explain main ideas. You can find details in the middle of paragraphs and in charts.

# Reading Books of Fiction

You can use a strategy like the **preview, read, reflect** strategy on this page when you are reading fiction. Short stories and novels are two kinds of fiction you will probably be reading.

## Preview, Read, Reflect (PRR)

 ### Preview

- Notice the title and author of the book.
- Look at the names of the chapters.
- Enjoy the pictures.
- Then think of some things that may happen to the characters in this story.

 ### Read

- Read part of the story or book.
- As you read, stop and ask yourself, "What is happening now?" If you're not sure what is happening, keep reading or go back and reread a part that is not clear.
- Predict what may happen next.
- Continue reading and predicting until you finish the book.

 ### Reflect

- After you finish reading the story, think about what the characters experienced and learned.
- Did you like the ending? Why or why not?

# Facts About Fiction

Short stories and novels are called fiction. This list will help you whether you are reading a story or writing your own story.

- A **character** is a person or an animal in a story. The characters are usually the most important part of the story.

- The **setting** describes where and when the story takes place.

- The **problem** presents something that is wrong or troublesome, especially for the main character. Problems (also called "conflicts") can be caused by the main character, another character, or nature.

- An **event** is something that happens to the characters of the story. It is sometimes called an episode.

- The **plot** is the sequence of events in the story. To identify the plot, ask, "What happened in this story?"

- The **solution** is the main character's way of dealing with the problem.

- The **theme** is the message or lesson a reader learns from the story. Each reader can "hear" a different message and learn a different lesson from the same story.

# Vocabulary and Spelling Skills

# Building

# Vocabulary Skills

You see and hear new words just about every day. Your teacher might use a word you've never heard before. You might see a new word in a book. Once in a while, you might hear a new word on TV.

## What's New?

Building a great sandwich takes special attention. So does building a great vocabulary. When you know a lot of words, it's easier to say exactly what you want to say. This chapter will help you do that.

# Learning New Words

### 1 Read, read, read!

The best way to learn new words is to read a lot. Books, magazines, newspapers, Web sites—read anything and everything!

### 2 Check nearby words.

The words that come before and after a new word may help you find its meaning. Check out the following sentence:

> The animal expert talked about herons, cranes, and ibises.

Ibises? That's probably a new word for you! Look at the words that come before it. Herons and cranes are both long-legged birds. Ibises are probably long-legged birds, too.

Here's another sentence with a new word:

> At work, my mom uses a microscope to look at germs.

A microscope is an instrument for looking at very small things. What words in this sentence help you know that?

## 3 Keep a new-word notebook.

Make a special notebook for new words. Write the meaning and a sentence for each new word.

### Vocabulary

| Word | Meaning | Sentence |
| --- | --- | --- |
| ibis | long-legged wading bird | The ibis is a wading bird with a long, curved bill. |
| microscope | an instrument used to see very small objects | Carla's mom uses a microscope to study water pollution. |

## 4 Practice using new words.

Try using new words in your writing and speaking. For example, each week, choose one new word from your notebook. Then think of ways to use it when writing or talking to friends and family. Using the word will help you remember it.

## 5 Look up the word in a dictionary.

Use a **dictionary** to look up new words. The dictionary gives you the meanings for each word plus much more.

**Syllable Division** ● A dictionary shows you how a word is divided into syllables. (Look for the heavy black dots.)

**Guide Words** ● These are the words at the top of the page. They tell you where you are according to the alphabet.

**Spelling** ● The dictionary shows you the correct spelling for a word. It also shows whether a word should be capitalized or not.

**Pronunciation** ● A dictionary shows you how a word should be said, or pronounced. The pronunciation is given in parentheses ( ). The pronunciation key at the bottom of the dictionary page will help you, too.

**Parts of Speech** ● The dictionary tells you if a word is a *noun,* a *verb,* an *adjective,* or another part of speech.

**Word History** ● Some words have stories about their history—where they came from and their early meaning.

**Synonyms** ● For some words, the dictionary lists other words that mean the same thing.

**Meaning** ● Some words have only one meaning. Some words have many meanings.

# Sample Dictionary Page

**Guide words**

**haven't ➤ haystack**

**How the word is used**

**haven't** Contraction of "have not."
**have•n't** (hăv´ənt) ◇ *contraction*

**havoc** *noun* Very great destruction: *The hurricane created havoc throughout the coastal area.*
**hav•oc** (hăv´ək) ◇ *noun*

**hawk¹** *noun* A large bird with a short, hooked bill, strong claws, and keen eyesight. Hawks catch small birds and animals for food.
**hawk¹** (hôk) ◇ *noun, plural* **hawks**

**hawk²** *verb* To offer for sale by shouting in the street; peddle.
**hawk²** (hôk) ◇ *verb* **hawked, hawking**

**Word history**

### Word History

**hawk¹, hawk²**
**Hawk¹** comes from the old English name for this bird.
**Hawk²** is a verb made from *hawker,* an old word for a person who peddles items on the street.

**Spelling**

**hawthorn** *noun* A thorny shrub or tree having white, red, or pinkish flowers and red berries.
**haw•thorn** (hô´ thôrn´) ◇ *noun, plural* **hawthorns**

**hay** *noun* Grass, clover, and other plants, cut and dried and used as fodder.
**hay** (hā) *noun*

**Pronunciation**

•)) *These sound alike:* **hay, hey**

**hay fever** *noun* An allergy caused by plant pollen that floats in the air. Hay fever causes sneezing, a runny nose, and itching, watery eyes.

**Meaning**

**hayloft** *noun* An upper floor in a barn or stable for storing hay.
**hay•loft** (hā´ lôft´) ◇ *noun, plural* **haylofts**

**hayride** *noun* A ride taken for pleasure in a wagon partly filled with hay.

**Syllable division**

**hay•ride** (hā´ rīd´) ◇ *noun, plural* **hayrides**

**haystack** *noun* A large pile of hay that is left outdoors during the winter.

**Pronunciation key**

**hay•stack** (hā´ stăk´) ◇ *noun, plural* **haystacks**

| | | | | | |
|---|---|---|---|---|---|
| ă pat | ĕ pet | î fierce | oi oil | ŭ cut | ə ago, item |
| ā pay | ē be | ŏ pot | ŏŏ book | û fur | pencil |
| â care | ĭ pit | ō go | ōō boot | th bath | atom |
| ä father | ī ride | ô paw, for | ou out | *th* bathe | circus |

## 6 Use a thesaurus.

A **thesaurus** is a book of words and their synonyms. Synonyms are words that mean almost the same thing. For example, if you look up *walk* in a thesaurus, you may find *stroll, hike,* and *step.* A thesaurus may also list antonyms for some words. Antonyms are words that mean the opposite.

**Look for the Right Word** ● Let's say you use a thesaurus to find just the right word for *hit* in the following sentence:

Josie _____ the ball over the shortstop's head.

Look up the word *hit* as you would in a dictionary. (As you can see below, it is located between *history* and *hitch.*)

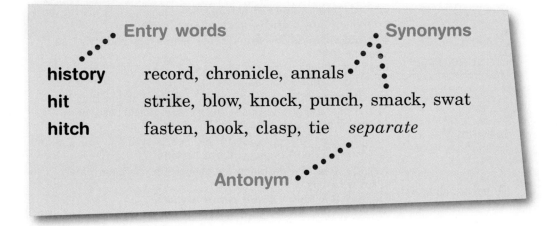

Entry words                    Synonyms

**history**    record, chronicle, annals

**hit**        strike, blow, knock, punch, smack, swat

**hitch**      fasten, hook, clasp, tie   *separate*

Antonym

**Choose the Right Word** ● Review the list of synonyms and choose the word that works best for your sentence. In the example, the best word seems to be *smack:*

Josie <u>smacked</u> the ball over the shortstop's head.

# 7 Divide the word into parts.

You can figure out the meanings of new words by learning about the three word parts:

**Root:** A root is the main part of a word. This part is also called the *word base.*

**Prefix:** A prefix comes before the root and changes its meaning.

**Suffix:** A suffix comes after the root and changes its meaning.

unicyclist

**Root:** cycl (meaning *wheel*)

**Prefix:** uni (meaning *one*)

**Suffix:** ist (meaning *someone who does something*)

## A Closer Look

Knowing the meaning of "uni" and "ist" helps you figure out the new word made from *cycl.* Let's see how:

- If you know that the prefix "uni" means "one," then *unicycle* must mean a cycle with one wheel.

- Also, if you know that the suffix "ist" means "someone who does something," then a *cyclist* must be someone who rides a cycle.

- Finally, a *unicyclist* must be someone who rides a cycle with one wheel.

# Using Prefixes, Suffixes, Roots

It sure would be nice to have a 3-D Super Deluxe Wordmaster Machine. By pulling a few levers, you could make all kinds of new words. And by pushing a few buttons, you could find out what they mean. Sorry, there is no machine like that.

## The Next Best Thing

On the next nine pages, you will find a dictionary of common prefixes, suffixes, and roots. This special dictionary will help you build new words into your vocabulary. Since there are no levers to pull or buttons to push, try working with your new words in a notebook. (See page 211.)

A **root** is a word base:
**graph**

A **prefix** comes before a root:
<u>auto</u>graph

A **suffix** comes after a root:
autograph<u>ed</u>

# Prefixes

**Prefixes** are word parts that come at the beginning of a word, before the root.  They often change the meaning of the root.

**amphi (both)**

**amphibian** (an animal that lives both on land and in water)

**anti (against)**

**antibody** (part of the blood that works against germs)

**astro (star, space)**

**astronaut** (space traveler)
**astronomy** (study of the stars and outer space)

**auto (self)**

**automatic** (working by itself)

**bi (two)**

**bicycle** (two-wheeled cycle)

**cent (hundred)**

**century** (100 years)

**ex (out)**

**exit** (to go out)

**hemi, semi (half)**

**hemisphere** (half of a sphere)
**semicircle** (half of a circle)

# Prefixes

**micro (very small)**

**microscope** (tool for looking at very small things)

**mono (one; *also see* uni)**

**monorail** (train that runs on one track)

**non (no, not; *also see* un)**

**nonfiction** (factual)

**oct (eight)**

**octopus** (a sea animal with eight armlike tentacles)

**pre (before)**

**predict** (to tell about something before it happens)

**quad (four)**

**quadruped** (an animal having four feet)

**sub (under)**

**submarine** (an underwater ship)

**tri (three)**

**triangle** (shape with three sides)

**un (not; *also see* non)**

**unhealthy** (not healthy)

**uni (one; *also see* mono)**

**unique** (one of a kind)

# Suffixes

**Suffixes** are word parts that come at the end of a word, after the root. They often change the meaning of the root.

### able (can do)
changeable (can change)

### ed (past tense)
learned (to learn something in the past)

### er (a person who)
baker (a person who bakes)

### er (more)
friendlier (more friendly)

### ess (female)
lioness (a female lion)

### est (most)
funniest (most funny)

### ful (full)
helpful (full of help)

### ing (doing something)
talking (doing what it is to talk)

### ist (a person who)
pianist (a person who plays piano)

# Suffixes

## less (without)

careless (without care)

## ly (in some manner)

completely (in a complete manner)

## ment (act of)

movement (the act of moving)

## ology (study of)

biology (study of living things)

## s, es (plural, more than one)

trees (more than one tree)

## sion, tion (state of)

expansion (state of expanding)
addition (state of adding)

## y (having)

rosy (having a rose color)

# Roots

A **root** is the main part of a word. It helps you understand the word's meaning. The next five pages list some common roots.

### agri (field)

**agriculture** (growing things in fields; farming)

### anni, annu (year)

**anniversary** (the same date on which an event happened)
**biannual** (twice a year)

### aud (hear)

**auditorium** (a place to hear something)

### biblio (book)

**bibliography** (list of books)

### bio (life)

**biography** (writing about a person's life)

### chron (time)

**chronological** (the time order in which things happened)

### cycl, cyclo (wheel, circular)

**bicycle** (a vehicle with two wheels)
**cyclone** (a circular wind)

### dem (people)

**democracy** (government by the people)

# Roots

### dent, dont (tooth)

**denture** (false teeth)
**orthodontist** (a person who straightens teeth)

### derm (skin)

**dermatology** (the study of skin)

### dynam (power)

**dynamite** (powerful explosive)

### equi (equal)

**equinox** (day and night of equal length)

### flex (bend)

**flexible** (able to bend)

### geo (earth)

**geography** (study of the earth)

### gram (letter, writing)

**telegram** (a letter sent from far away)
**grammar** (rules for writing)

### graph (write)

**autograph** (to write one's own name)

### hab, habit (live)

**inhabit** (to live in)

### hydr (water)

**hydrant** (a place where firefighters get water to fight fires)

### leg (law)

**legal** (related to the law)

### log, ology (word, study)

**prologue** (words that come before the main part of a book)
**zoology** (study of animals)

### magn (great; *also see* mega)

**magnify** (to make something appear larger)

### man (hand)

**manicure** (to groom the hands)

### mar (sea)

**marine** (related to the sea)

### max (greatest)

**maximum** (the greatest amount possible)

### mega (great, huge; *also see* magn)

**megaphone** (instrument that makes a sound louder)

### mem (remember)

**memo** (a note to remember something)

### meter (measure)

**thermometer** (an instrument that measures heat)

# Roots

**migr (move)**

**migrant** (one who moves from one place to another)

**min (small, less)**

**minimum** (the smallest amount possible)
**minus** (less)

**multi (many)**

**multicultural** (including many cultures)

**narr (tell)**

**narrative** (writing that tells a story)

**neg (no)**

**negative** (meaning or saying no)

**ped (foot; *also see* pod)**

**pedal** (an instrument that is operated with the foot)

**phon (sound)**

**telephone** (a way sound travels)

**photo (light)**

**photograph** (a picture formed by light)

**pod (foot; *also see* ped)**

**tripod** (an object with three feet or legs)

**port (carry)**

**portable** (able to be carried)

### scope (see)
**otoscope** (an instrument used for seeing inside the ear)

### scribe (write)
**inscribe** (to write or carve letters onto something)

### spec (look)
**inspect** (to look at carefully)

### sphere (ball)
**spherical** (having the shape of a ball)

### sum (highest)
**summit** (the highest point, top)

### tele (far)
**telescope** (an instrument for seeing things that are far away)

### therm (heat)
**thermal** (related to heat)

### tox (poison)
**toxic** (poisonous)

### vid, vis (see)
**video** (the part of an electronic program that can be seen)
**supervise** (to oversee, or to look over)

### zo (animal)
**zoology** (the study of animals)

# Becoming a Better Speller

Do you realize that when you can spell one word, you have a head start on learning to spell many others? That's right. For example, if you can spell *night*, you'll find it easier to spell *light*, *lightly*, *lighthouse*, and *lightning*.

## Basic Steps

There are spelling rules to help you, too. (The tricky part is that some words just don't fit the rules.) In this chapter, we will tell you four ways to become a better speller:

**1** Use strategies to help you spell.

**2** Make a spelling dictionary.

**3** Proofread for spelling.

**4** Learn some basic spelling rules.

# 1 Use strategies to help you spell.

## Use your senses.

- Look at the word and listen as you say it.
- Cover the word. Try to "see" it in your mind.
- Write the word from memory.
- Check the spelling.
- If the word is misspelled, try again.

## Use a saying.

- A fri**end** sticks with you to the **end**.
  (This saying helps you remember that
  the *e* goes after the *i* in the word *friend*.)

## Think of similar words.

- **tw**o **tw**in **tw**enty    **tow** **tow**ard

## Use an acrostic.

- **Arithmetic**
  **A** **r**at **i**n **t**he **h**ouse **m**ight **e**at **t**he **i**ce **c**ream.
  (Each letter of the word you want to
  remember begins a word in a sentence.)

Say the acrostic for "arithmetic." As you say it, write down the first letter of each word. You've spelled the word! Arithmetic!

## Make a spelling dictionary.

In a small notebook, put one letter of the alphabet at the top of each page. (**A** goes at the top of the first page, **B** goes at the top of the second page, and so on.) Each time you learn a new word, write it in your spelling dictionary.

Next to each new word, write as many word relatives as you can think of. For example, *nights, nightly, nightmare, nightfall,* and *nightstand* are word relatives for *night.*

## Proofread for spelling.

Proofreading for spelling is one of the last things you do before you call your writing finished. When you're not sure of a spelling, circle the word. Then check the spelling in a dictionary or in your handbook. (See pages 312-315 for a spelling list.)

## Learn some basic spelling rules.

Rules can help you spell many words. But remember that there are **exceptions** to the rules. (An exception is a word that doesn't fit the rule.)

### Silent E

If a word ends with a silent **e**, drop the **e** before adding an ending that begins with a vowel, like **-ed** or **-ing**.

**share** changes to **shared**, **sharing**

**care** changes to **cared**, **caring**

## Words Ending in Y

When you write the plurals of words that end in **y,** change the **y** to **i** and add **es.** If the word ends in **ey,** just add **s.**

> **puppy** changes to **puppies**
> **turkey** changes to **turkeys**
> **pony** changes to **ponies**
> **donkey** changes to **donkeys**

## Consonant Ending

When a one-syllable word with a short vowel needs an ending like **-ed** or **-ing,** the final consonant is usually doubled. *Exception:* Do not double the consonant for words ending in **x,** as in *boxed* or *boxing.*

> **stop** changes to **stopped, stopping**
> **swim** changes to **swimming, swimmer**
> **quit** changes to **quitter, quitting**
> **star** changes to **starry, starring**

## I Before E

Use **i** before **e** except after **c** or when these letters "say" $\bar{a}$, as in *neighbor* or *weigh.*

- *i* before *e* words: **friend, piece, relief, believe, audience, chief, fierce**
- exceptions to *i* before *e* rule: **either, neither, their, height, weird**

# Viewing, Speaking, and Listening Skills

# Learning to View

Watching television and browsing the Web can be fun. You have thousands of choices for entertainment and information. Some of these programs and sites are very good, but many of them are not.

This chapter gives you tips for viewing programs and sites to get the most from them. It also gives you the real story behind many ads and commercials.

# Viewing News Programs

Some **news programs** cover news in your community and state. Other programs cover national and world news. Here are three things to remember about the news.

 **News programs can't show you everything that happens each day.**

That would take too much time. Instead, the program directors decide what to show you.

 **News programs don't always tell the whole story.**

The reporters and directors decide how much to tell you about each event.

 **News reporters don't always know all of the facts.**

## Covering the Basic Facts

A good news story should tell you all the basic facts:

| | |
|---|---|
| **Who?** | Third grader Leslie Smythe |
| **What?** | rode her bike around the world |
| **When?** | last week. |
| **Where?** | She started out in Philadelphia. |
| **Why?** | She wanted to see if she could do it. |
| **How?** | Leslie's dad is an airline pilot. Leslie and her bike were on an airplane! |

**Web Connection:** These reminders about news programs also apply to news stories reported on the Web.

# Viewing Educational Programs

**TV specials** and many educational videos give information about one subject. They can be about people, places, animals, or events. You've probably watched many nature specials. You may also have seen special programs about famous events and strange creatures like Big Foot and the Loch Ness Monster. Here are some tips that will help you with your viewing.

## Before Viewing

- Before watching a special program, decide what you would like to know about the subject.
- If your teacher gives you questions to answer, make sure you understand all of them.

## During Viewing

- As you watch the program, write down a few key words to help you remember important ideas.
- Write down any questions you have.

## After Viewing

- Talk about the program with someone else who has watched it. Answer your teacher's questions.
- Try writing your thoughts about the program in a journal.

**Web Connection:** Use these same tips when you view a feature story on a Web site.

# Viewing Advertisements

If you watch TV regularly, you see about 300 commercials every week! The people who write those commercials use many different selling methods to make you believe that you should buy their products.

## Selling Methods

- **Bandwagon** Some commercials show a group of people enjoying a certain product. After watching this type of ad, you may feel like "hopping on the bandwagon" by buying and using the product, too.

- **Name-Calling** Instead of just saying that a product is good, some commercials say that other brands are not as good. This name-calling says, "Our stuff is better than all of the other stuff."

- **Famous Faces** Putting famous people in commercials helps sell products. *Hotrod Jones wears _____ shoes so you should, too.*

- **Facts Plus** A commercial may use facts or surveys to sell a product. *Nine out of ten kids say _____ is their favorite bubble gum.* So you better try some yourself!

- **Before and After** Let's say a commercial shows a student having a bad day at school. Then we see the same student smiling after someone hands him a certain candy bar. This is the old before-and-after idea: Our product will make you happy.

# Tips for Viewing Web Sites

Like television, the Web is a source of information and entertainment. The Web includes both personal and professional sites. These sites are filled with facts and opinions about millions of topics. It's up to you to decide if you can trust this information. Use the following points to help:

- **Check to see who publishes the Web site.** Web sites can belong to government offices, businesses, schools, organizations, or ordinary citizens (even kids). When you read what a site has to say, it is good to know who published it. You can usually find the publisher's name on the home page.

- **Check for current dates.** Some sites have all the latest news. Other sites are out-of-date. Look for dates on Web pages (usually at the bottom) to learn how old the information is at that site.

- **Check other sources.** It's always best to compare more than one source. Don't forget to check books and magazines, too.

# Learning to Listen

You spend a lot of your time listening. You listen to your teacher, your friends, your parents—even your TV! But listening is not the same as hearing. You may hear your brother talking on the phone, but you're not listening unless you pay attention and think about what he's saying.

| Hearing | Listening |
|---|---|
| Two friends talking | A friend talking to you |
| Music on the radio | A favorite song on the radio |
| The TV in the next room | The TV you're watching |

## Are You Listening?

**Listening** is a great way to learn things. The better you listen, the more you'll learn. But being a good listener is not easy. For example, you can't daydream and listen at the same time. You must "stay tuned" to what a speaker is saying.

# Good-Listener Checklist

✔ **Look at the person who is speaking.**

Don't stare out the window.
Your mind goes where your eyes go.

✔ **Listen with your eyes as well as your ears.**

Try to decide how the person feels about
his or her ideas. Watch the *body language*—
what the speaker does with his or her hands,
face, and voice.

✔ **Listen for key words.**

- The **biggest** planet is Jupiter.
- The planet **farthest** from the sun is Pluto.

✔ **Think about what is being said.**

What do the speaker's ideas mean to you?

✔ **Ask questions when you don't understand.**

Be polite. Ask questions when the speaker
pauses or asks for questions.

✔ **Take notes or make drawings.**

Don't try to write down too much. List the
most important ideas.

# Performing Poems

At Randall School, Lola and her classmates enjoyed watching some actors performing poems. The actors moved around and made the poems come alive. All of the students wanted the show to go on and on. They had no idea that poetry could be so much fun.

## Students Onstage

Lola and some of her classmates wondered about performing poems themselves. They knew many poems and had written some of their own. (And they felt like sharing their poems with their classmates!) In this chapter, you can learn how to perform your own poems.

# Moving Poetry from Page to Stage

Use the ideas on the following pages, and your poetry performance will be a smash hit!

 **Form a team.**

Get together with a few classmates. A good team size is two, three, or four performers.

 **Find poems to perform.**

Have you or your partners written any poems? If so, look them over. Look through books of poems, too—from your classroom, the library, or home.

**Collect different types of poems.** Collect funny ones, clever ones, and serious ones. Take turns reading the poems out loud.

**Choose the right poem.** Poems that have a lot of action are easiest to perform, so consider those first. Poems that tell about feelings are harder, but try performing one for a challenge.

**Script the poem.**

After you have chosen a poem, divide it into speaking parts. This is called **scripting**.

**Original Poem** ● Let's use Treva LaCosta's short poem "All Aboard!" to show you how to script. First read the poem, and then see how it was made into a script.

**All Aboard!**
Come passengers small and passengers tall,
Take your seats, and pull in your feet.
All aboard, tickets please!
It's not a plane or a boat with a sail.
**Today we're riding a monorail!**
All aboard, tickets please!

**Scripted Poem** ● In the scripted poem, there are three performers: two narrators and a conductor.

| | |
|---|---|
| **Narrator 1:** | Come passengers small |
| **Narrator 2:** | and passengers tall, |
| **Narrator 1:** | Take your seats, |
| **Narrator 2:** | and pull in your feet. |
| **Conductor:** | All aboard, tickets please! |
| **Narrator 1:** | It's not a plane or a boat with a sail. |
| **All:** | Today we're riding a monorail! |
| **Conductor:** | All aboard, tickets please! |

To script your poem, you must decide how many speaking parts to include. People, animals, or things can speak.

**Score the poem.**

Next you must **score** the poem. That means naming feelings and movements for different lines of your script. You don't need feelings and movements for every line. Sometimes you can simply say parts of the poem.

|  |  | *Feeling* | **Movement** |
|---|---|---|---|
| **Narrator 1:** | Come passengers small | *(soft)* | **wave hand to come** |
| **Narrator 2:** | and passengers tall, | *(loud)* | **stand up on tiptoes** |
| **Narrator 1:** | Take your seats, | *(excited)* | **point down** |
| **Narrator 2:** | and pull in your feet. | *(silly)* | **move feet** |
| **Conductor:** | All aboard, tickets please! | *(serious)* | **hands to mouth** |
| **Narrator 1:** | It's not a plane | | **shake head** |
| **Narrator 2:** | or a boat with a sail. | | |
| **All:** | Today we're riding a monorail! | *(excited)* | **wave arms and jump** |
| **Conductor:** | All aboard, tickets please! | *(serious)* | **hands to mouth** |

**5** **Perform your poem.**

After you have scripted and scored your poem, start reading it out loud. Keep practicing until everyone knows his or her lines. Then get ready to perform.

# Performance Tips

- **Act confident.** Stand straight or sit tall. Don't fidget.

- **Face your audience.** As a rule, never turn your back to the audience, not even a little.

- **Introduce the poem and the poet.** Before your performance, stand shoulder to shoulder. Together, announce the title of the poem and the poet's name. Then move to your starting positions.

- **Use your "outside" voices.** This is the voice you'll need so everyone can hear you! Remember to add the right feelings and movements when you speak.

- **Exit quietly.** When your performance is over, pause for a moment, take a bow, and return to your seats.

# Encore! Encore!

Use the poem on this page for an encore (an additional performance). You and your team can add your own feelings and movements to the poem.

### What Is a Poem?
#### by Allan Wolf

**Rocket:** A Poem can be a rocket—ZOOM!—that I can ride up to the sky.

**Bird-watcher:** A Poem can be a secret room where I can watch the birds fly by.

**Firecracker:** A Poem can be loud fireworks—BOOM—all whoosh and bang and sparks and fun.

**Flower:** A Poem can be a flower bloom that holds itself up to the sun.

**Bird-watcher:** A Poem can whisper,

**Firecracker:** shout,

**Rocket:** and play.

**Flower:** A Poem can dance and sing.

**All:** I never realized a Poem could be so many things!

# Giving Short Talks

Do you and a friend ever sit and talk about a subject you're interested in? Has someone told you how to do something—like fix a flat tire on your bike? Sharing information like that is called conversation. But, when you share the same information with a group, it's called a short talk (or a speech).

## Learning by Doing

Giving talks becomes easier with practice. Who knows? You may even start to like it and someday become a famous talker. (Know any famous talkers?) This chapter will help you learn all about giving a short talk—from picking a subject to practicing what you will say.

# Pick a subject.

First, pick a subject that really interests you. Here are some examples:

> Something that happened to you:
>    I broke my arm.
> Something you like to do:
>    I love skateboarding!
> Something you read about:
>    I just read a book about whales.

Then write about your subject in one sentence. Everything in your talk should be about that sentence.

# Learn about your topic.

You can learn about your subject by remembering, reading, and asking questions.

**Remembering** ● List everything that you remember and know about the subject. Fill a whole page with ideas!

**Reading** ● Learn more by reading about your subject. Ask your librarian for books and magazines that discuss your subject. Take notes as you read.

**Asking Questions** ● Talk to people who know a lot about your subject. If your subject is skateboarding, you could talk to someone who sells skateboards. Try it. It's called an interview. (See pages 252-255 for help.)

## Know your purpose.

Decide why you want to talk about your subject. This will be your purpose. Do you want to . . .

- share the important details about an event,
- help your listeners learn something new,
- make them laugh or feel sad, or
- get them to agree with you about something?

## Plan your talk.

Next, you must plan your talk and decide which ideas you will include. Think about what your audience, or listeners, would like to hear. Here are some tips to get you going:

### To BEGIN your talk . . .

- say something interesting or surprising to get your listeners' attention, and
- tell what your subject is.

### In the MIDDLE of your talk . . .

- give interesting facts about the subject, and
- tell how you feel about it.

### To END your talk . . .

- remind listeners what your subject is, and
- repeat an important idea about it.

# 5 Write your talk.

To help you prepare for your talk, write it down on paper. There are two ways to do this. You can write your talk word for word on a full sheet of paper. (See page 249.) Or you can write the main ideas on note cards. (See the sample note cards below.)

# Sample Note Cards

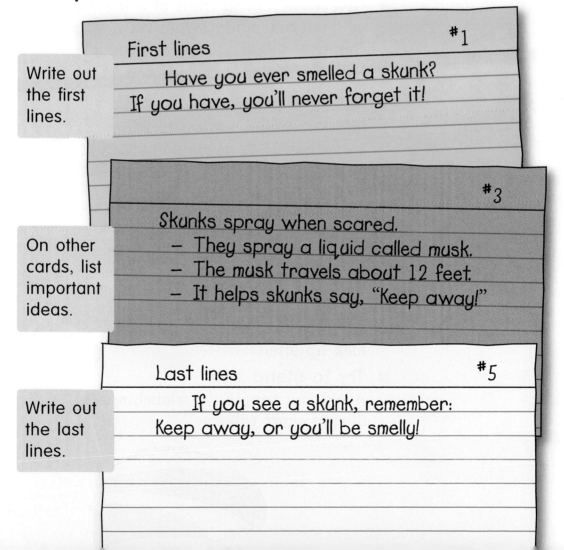

Write out the first lines.

**#1** First lines
Have you ever smelled a skunk?
If you have, you'll never forget it!

On other cards, list important ideas.

**#3**
Skunks spray when scared.
 — They spray a liquid called musk.
 — The musk travels about 12 feet.
 — It helps skunks say, "Keep away!"

Write out the last lines.

**#5** Last lines
If you see a skunk, remember:
Keep away, or you'll be smelly!

## Practice giving your talk.

If you're using note cards, practice saying the ideas listed on each card. Do this over and over until you can repeat all of the ideas easily. If you have written your talk out word for word, practice reading it or try to memorize it. Here are more practicing tips:

- Start practicing early, at least two days before your talk.
- Give your talk in front of a few friends or family members. Ask them what they think.
- Follow the tips listed in step 7 below.

**T/P** As you practice, think about what visual aids you might use—a picture, a chart, a recording. (See pages 250-251.)

## Give your talk.

When you finally give your talk, keep these tips in mind:

- **Speak loudly, clearly, and slowly.**
- **Look at your audience.**
  If you're reading your talk, look up often.
- **Try to stand still.**
  Avoid foot tapping or slouching during short talks!

# Sample Short Talk

Here's a short talk written by Jana Taylor.

**Name the subject in an interesting way.**

**Give interesting facts.**

**Repeat the most important idea.**

## Skunks

Have you ever smelled a skunk? If you have, you'll never forget it!

If you've seen a skunk, it was probably a striped one. They have white stripes on their backs, and they're about the same size as a cat. But there are also spotted skunks. Spotted skunks are very small. They weigh only about one pound. When they spray, they stand up on their front paws—like doing a handstand!

Skunks only spray when they're scared. They spray a liquid called musk. Musk smells awful and can travel about 12 feet. It's the skunk's way of saying, "Keep away!" It works, too!

When you get sprayed by a skunk, you smell really bad. And it's hard to get the smell off. Our dog scared a skunk in our yard. My mom poured tomato juice all over the dog. For some reason, tomato juice helps get rid of the skunk smell.

If you see a skunk, remember: Keep away, or you'll be smelly!

# Making a Multimedia Slide Show

You can use a computer drawing program to help "dress up" your talk with pictures. You can also use a multimedia program (like *Hyperstudio*™, *Kid Pix*™, or *Power Point*™) to turn your pictures into a "slide show."

 **Plan your slide show.**

Use your note cards or written speech to make a storyboard. On a piece of paper, draw a box for each main idea in your talk. Here's a storyboard for the short talk "Skunks."

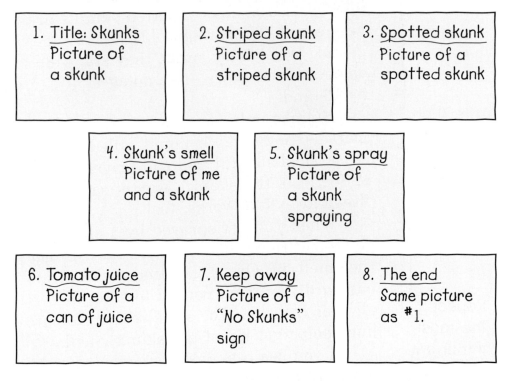

| | | |
|---|---|---|
| 1. Title: Skunks<br>Picture of a skunk | 2. Striped skunk<br>Picture of a striped skunk | 3. Spotted skunk<br>Picture of a spotted skunk |
| 4. Skunk's smell<br>Picture of me and a skunk | 5. Skunk's spray<br>Picture of a skunk spraying | |
| 6. Tomato juice<br>Picture of a can of juice | 7. Keep away<br>Picture of a "No Skunks" sign | 8. The end<br>Same picture as #1. |

**TIP** Visit <www.thewritesource.com/mm.htm> to view this slide show.

## Make your pictures.

Use the computer to draw the pictures for your slide show. (You can also print out copies of your pictures to use when giving your talk without a computer.)

## Link your pictures.

Use a multimedia program to make each picture a slide. You can add sounds, but don't let them distract from the message. Ask your teacher for help with sounds, timing, and "transitions" (the change from slide to slide).

## Practice your talk.

Practice giving your talk with the slide show. Have a friend or family member listen. Ask them for suggestions.

## Give your talk.

Stand next to the computer as you give your talk. Remember to look at your listeners as you speak. (Also remember the tips for giving your talk at the bottom of page 248.)

# Learning to
# Interview

One day Gabi Ruiz had an assignment. Everyone in her class had to write a report about what they wanted to be when they grew up. Gabi's uncle is a sportswriter, and she thought it sounded exciting. But she wasn't sure she really knew enough about her uncle's job. She needed more information. So Gabi called her uncle to ask for an interview.

If you can't meet with the person you want to interview, you may be able to ask your questions over the phone.

# What Is an Interview?

An **interview** is a special kind of conversation between two people. One person asks questions, and the other person answers them. It is a way to collect information. The answers can be used in reports or short talks. This chapter will help you get ready for your first interview.

## Before the Interview

### Decide what you want to learn from the interview.

- Think about what your audience might want to know.
- List questions that will help you get all of this information.
- Begin your questions with words like *how, what,* and *why.* You can learn a lot by asking questions that begin with these words.

### Find out who knows a lot about your topic.

- Call that person and ask for an interview.
- Identify the project you are working on.
- Set a time and place to meet.

### Gather your materials.

- Your list of questions
- Two or three pencils
- A notebook
- A tape recorder (if you want to use one)

## During the Interview

**Introduce yourself and get ready for the interview.**

- Remind the person who you are and what your interview is about.
- If you have a tape recorder, ask if you may use it.

**Ask your questions.**

- Be sure your questions are clear and ask for details rather than a simple "yes" or "no."
- If an answer is unclear, ask for more information.

**Listen carefully and take notes.**

- Write down the key ideas and details.
- When you take notes, politely say, "I want to write that down." The person will stop talking so you can write.
- Ask the person to spell names you are unsure of.

## After the Interview

**Read your notes.**

- Add any details that come to mind.
- If you used a tape recorder, listen to the tape.

**Share what you learned.**

- Write a report or give a short talk about your interview.
- Use the exact words of the speaker if you are trying to make an important point.

# An Interview in Action

Here are questions and answers from Gabi's interview.

1. Why did you decide to become a sportswriter?
   loves sports and writing
2. How did you become a sportswriter?
   went to college, learned how to watch games, learned a lot more on the job

## Sample Report from an Interview

### Sportswriting

Someday, I want to be a sportswriter like my uncle, Joe Cotto. He says you have to love sports and writing to be a sportswriter.

It is not easy to become a sportswriter! First, you must go to college to learn how to be a reporter. You must also learn how to watch sports events carefully.

After college, once you have a job, you learn a lot more. My uncle said, "You'll probably get your first job in the town where you live. If you're a good writer, you may be able to get a job in a bigger city. You may be able to interview famous athletes." I'd like that.

# Telling Stories

Mya remembers her grandmother telling wonderful made-up stories. Sometimes the stories were funny or sad. Sometimes they were scary. But the greatest thing about the stories was how her grandmother told them. Maybe there is someone in your family who can tell great stories. Maybe that person could be you! To become a good storyteller, you can do two easy things.

Read a lot of stories so you can choose the best ones to tell.

Practice as much as you can.

Stories
by G. Brothers

# Choosing a Story

Folktales, fairy tales, legends, and tall tales are all fun to tell. Choose a story you really like—one you can tell in about 5 minutes. Stories that repeat words or lines (like *The Three Billy Goats Gruff*) make good choices. Listeners like to hear special words repeated. It keeps them interested in the story.

# Learning the Story

## Read the Story Out Loud

Read the story out loud three or four times. Try to picture what is happening—as if you were watching a movie in your mind.

## Make Note Cards

**Write down the first and last sentences** of the story on separate note cards.

**Then write down ideas about the main events** of the story. Use a different index card for each event. (See the next two pages.)

**On some cards, add interesting words and actions** you could say or do.

- Mark words you want to say with special feeling.
- Add movements or sounds you want to make.

## Try to Memorize Your Story

You should be able to tell the story without looking at your notes!

# Sample Note Cards

On these two pages, you will find sample note cards for the story "Walking Catfish." (This story is on pages 260-261.) The first five cards and the very last one are included here.

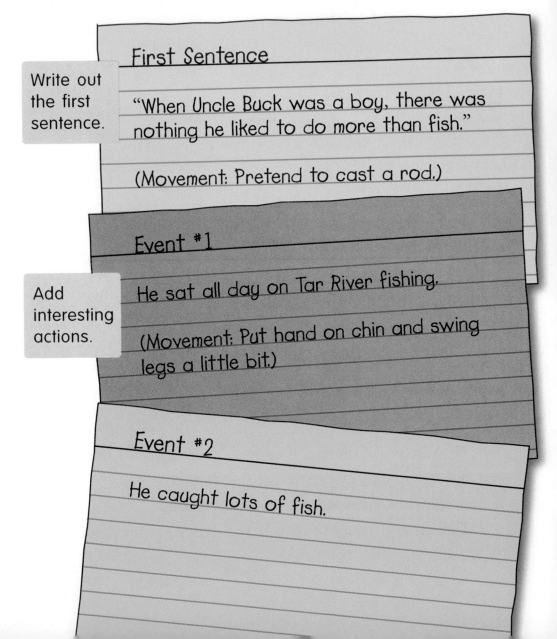

Write out the first sentence.

**First Sentence**

"When Uncle Buck was a boy, there was nothing he liked to do more than fish."

(Movement: Pretend to cast a rod.)

Add interesting actions.

**Event #1**

He sat all day on Tar River fishing.

(Movement: Put hand on chin and swing legs a little bit.)

**Event #2**

He caught lots of fish.

Event #3

Add interesting words to say.

He hung them all on a stringer, but one kept breathing hard.

(Say "Wooo-wheee" three times.)

Event #4

Buck put this fish in a water bucket and went inside for supper.

(Movement: Rub stomach.)

Write out the last sentence word for word.

Last Sentence

"Just goes to show, ya gotta let folks be what they're meant to be."

If you like "Walking Catfish," you could write the rest of the index cards. Then tell the story to someone who has never heard it.

# Professional *Sample*

## WALKING CATFISH
*Retold by Charles Temple*

When Uncle Buck was a boy, there was nothing he liked to do more than fish. Oh, he sat all day down on Tar River fishing. One July day, seemed like every time his bait hit the bottom, he felt a yank and pulled in a big, old catfish. He'd take it off the hook, being careful not to grab the spine, and throw it up on the bank.

Buck climbed up on the bank and commenced to hang those fish on the stringer. But one hardy fellow had no intention of ending up on Buck's dinner plate. He was hangin' there breathing hard: "Wooo-wheee. Wooo-wheee. Wooo-wheee."

So Buck put him into a bucket of water and went on inside to have his supper. Next morning he come outside and took that fish out of the bucket. He was still breathing: "Wooo-wheee. Wooo-wheee. Wooo-wheee."

So Buck decided to work with him a little. He left him out of that bucket a whole hour before he put him back in. The next day, he left him out all morning. Pretty soon that fish never went back in the water at all.

Buck didn't have a puppy, so he named that fish Jake, and taught him to follow along behind him. You should have seen Jake flopping along through the dust and gravel, still breathing: "Wooo-wheee. Wooo-wheee. Wooo-wheee."

Wasn't anywhere Buck went that Jake didn't follow. Well, it turned September and the school opened up. Buck trudged off down the road to third grade. But here come Jake flopping along behind: "Wooo-wheee. Wooo-wheee. Wooo-wheee."

"Go on home, Jake," shouted Buck. "Fish can't go to school."

But Jake came on. Buck crossed that old plank bridge and walked on up to the schoolhouse. When he looked back, Buck saw a plank busted out.

He looked down in the river, and there was Jake, thrashing about like to drown.

"Swim, Jake, swim!" Buck shouted. "You can do it, boy." Well, Jake took him a deep breath and dove down under the water. And you know what? Buck never saw that fish again.

Just goes to show, ya gotta let folks be what they're meant to be.

# Thinking Skills

# Using Graphic Organizers

Not much would happen in this life if things weren't organized. Coaches couldn't get their teams ready. Scientists couldn't make discoveries. Cooks couldn't plan meals. Students like you couldn't do their best writing and reading. And geese would never make it south!

## Gathering and Grouping Ideas

Do you want to gather your thoughts for writing a story? No problem. Make a cluster. Do you have to compare two things? Try a Venn diagram. Would you like to organize a lot of facts? Write an outline.

Clusters, diagrams, and outlines are called **graphic organizers.** They can help you gather and group ideas.

# Clustering Ideas

How can you gather details about a past event? You can list the details as you think of them. However, if you want to be more organized, you can **cluster** your ideas.

Begin clustering by writing the subject in the middle of the page. Then list related words around it. Circle and connect your words.

 Clustering can help you organize facts for a story, a report, a speech, and other projects, too.

## 2 Describing a Subject

How can you collect details to describe someone or something? Use a **describing wheel.** Write your subject in the middle of your wheel. List words about the subject around it.

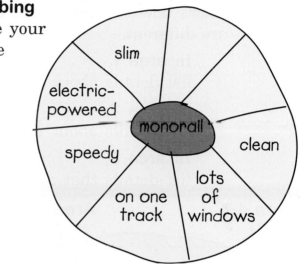

## 3 Answering the 5 W's

How can you tell if you know the important details about an event? Try answering the 5 W's.

## 4 Comparing Two Subjects

How can you compare two related subjects? Use a **Venn diagram.** This type of diagram shows how two things are alike, and how they are different.

In **area 1,**
list details about one of your subjects.

In **area 2,**
list details about the other subject.

In **area 3,**
list details that are true for both subjects.

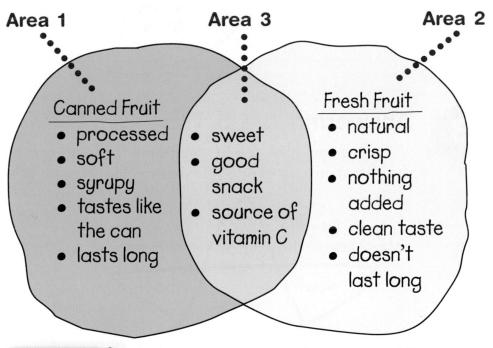

**Area 1**  **Area 3**  **Area 2**

Canned Fruit
- processed
- soft
- syrupy
- tastes like the can
- lasts long

- sweet
- good snack
- source of vitamin C

Fresh Fruit
- natural
- crisp
- nothing added
- clean taste
- doesn't last long

**On Track** To show how two subjects are alike, use the details in area **3**. To show how two subjects are different, use the details in areas **1** and **2**.

# 5 Outlining Your Ideas

How can you organize all of the information you have collected for a speech or report? Make an **outline**.

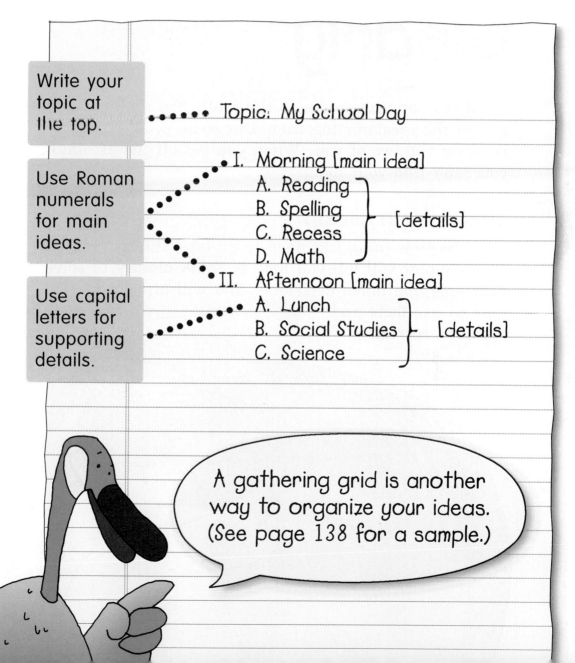

Write your topic at the top.

Use Roman numerals for main ideas.

Use capital letters for supporting details.

Topic: My School Day

I. Morning [main idea]
   A. Reading
   B. Spelling      } [details]
   C. Recess
   D. Math
II. Afternoon [main idea]
   A. Lunch
   B. Social Studies } [details]
   C. Science

A gathering grid is another way to organize your ideas. (See page 138 for a sample.)

# Thinking Clearly

Let's say that you're at the mall. You and your mom get on the escalator together. But some people squeeze in between the two of you. When you get off the escalator, you can't find your mom.

## Using Your Brain

The first thing you need to do is to think clearly. This chapter will tell you how to **think clearly** to solve problems and make decisions. You will also learn how to use facts and opinions correctly.

# Solving Problems

Imagine you're back at the mall. You've lost your mother. What do you do?

 **Name the problem.**

*I've lost my mother in a huge mall.*

 **List everything you know about the problem.**

*I won't find Mom by walking around.*
*I can see the food court where we like to eat.*
*Mom said, "If you get lost, don't talk to strangers."*

 **Think of ways to solve the problem.**

*I could just stay here and hope Mom finds me.*
*I could yell for help. But then I would have to talk to a stranger.*
*I could ask a worker at the food court for help.*

 **Choose the best plan and try it out.**

*I'll ask for help at the food court.*

**5** **Ask yourself: How did the plan work?**

*The worker at the food court called security.*
*They said my name on the loudspeaker, and Mom came!*

# Making Decisions

Sometimes you have a decision to make, and you're not sure what to do. Here's how to think clearly.

**1** **Write down what you have to decide.**
*Should I sign up for soccer or for swimming?*

**2** **List the facts.**
List your feelings and any questions you have.

| SOCCER | SWIMMING |
|---|---|
| Practices are on Thursday evenings. | Lessons are early Saturday. |
| Games are on Saturday afternoons. | I like to sleep late. |
| I won't know anybody! | My friends are taking lessons. |
| What will I learn? | It could be fun. |
| | What will I learn? |

**3** **Find the answers to your questions.**
Ask a parent or someone who has already played soccer or taken swimming lessons. Add their opinions to your list.

**4** **Make your decision.**
Put a ★ next to each "good" thing on your list. You might decide to do the activity with the most ★'s. Sometimes, one "good" thing—like being with your friends—might be more important to you than anything else. It's up to you!

# Using Facts and Opinions Correctly

Do you know the difference between a fact and an opinion? A **fact** tells about the way things are. An **opinion** tells about how a person thinks or feels. Facts and opinions are both important, but it's good to know the difference.

**Fact: Both dogs and cats can be pets.**

Opinion: I'd rather have a dog than a cat.

**Fact: Chocolate is made from cacao beans.**

Opinion: Chocolate tastes delicious.

## Fact vs. Opinion

Let's say your friend calls. She says, "It snowed last night. We shouldn't have school today!"

The first part of your friend's call is a **fact:** "It snowed last night." You can prove that statement by looking out the window. The second part is only her **opinion,** or feeling: "We shouldn't have school today." The fact is, school is open. Your mom said there were no school closings.

 Opinions are fine. (A "snow day" would have been great!) But it's always important to know the facts before you act or react.

# Sticking to the Facts

It's important to stick to the facts when you're trying to get someone to agree with you. It's also important to listen for facts when someone else wants you to agree with them! Here are some points to remember about facts.

## A statement is not a fact just because most people agree with it.

> A kangaroo would be a good classroom pet because almost everybody in the class thinks so.

No matter how many people share an opinion, it's still an opinion. It's not a fact. A kangaroo would be "hopping mad" in a classroom!

## A statement is not a fact if it is based only on feelings.

> A rattlesnake would be a good classroom pet because I think rattlesnakes are neat.

This statement is based on a feeling. It's not based on any facts about rattlesnakes. Here's a statement based on a fact: *A rattlesnake would not be a good classroom pet because a rattlesnake bite can be deadly.*

## A statement is not a fact if it is a half-truth.

> If you eat right and get enough rest, you won't catch a cold.

This is only half true. Eating right and getting enough rest can help you remain healthy and resist cold germs. Sometimes, however, even the healthiest person gets a cold. Here's how to turn this statement into a fact: *If you eat right and get enough rest, you will be less likely to catch a cold.*

## A statement is not a fact if it makes things seem worse (or better) than they really are.

> When a bee stings you, it hurts so much you go crazy.

This statement makes too much out of a bee sting. (Unless, of course, you are allergic to them.) A bee sting may hurt a little. But when you put medicine on it, it doesn't hurt for very long.

It can be hard to stick to the facts when you really want someone to agree with you. But don't get your own opinions mixed up with the facts.

# Writing to Learn

Writing is thinking on paper. A great place to do your writing (and thinking) is in a **learning log.** You can use a learning log in any class for any subject—math, science, history, and so on.

## Writing About Math

Paco's teacher asked, "What is multiplication?" Here's what Paco wrote in his learning log:

> Jan. 12    Multiplication is a lot like addition. Yesterday I bought 6 packs of gum. Each pack had 5 pieces in it. That gave me 30 pieces. I can get the answer by adding or multiplying.
>
> $$5 + 5 + 5 + 5 + 5 + 5 = 30$$
> $$6 \times 5 = 30$$

## Writing About Social Studies

As Rosie listened to her teacher read a biography of Abraham Lincoln, she had some questions. She wrote them down:

> Feb. 10    How did Abe Lincoln feel when his father got married again? How did his life change?

## Writing About Science

Leo wrote his observations of the pigeons nesting on his apartment windowsill:

Mar. 2   A pigeon made a nest on our windowsill. The nest is made of little sticks and leaves.

Mar. 5   There are two white eggs in the nest. One pigeon sits on the nest all day. Is it the mother?

# Tips for Writing to Learn

■ **When you learn something new, write down what you think about it.** This helps you figure out what you understand and what you still need to learn.

■ **Write down questions you have about a subject.** Don't worry about finding the answers right away. Read more about the subject; ask your teacher or classmates for help.

■ **List important words you are learning.** Also write the definitions of these words.

■ **Pretend you are telling a friend all about your reading.** Write down everything he or she needs to know to understand the subject.

■ **Draw pictures to make ideas clearer.** You could label a picture of the Big Dipper. The Big Dipper is a group of stars that is part of the Great Bear constellation.

# Learning Skills

# Completing
# Assignments

Whether you have one big assignment to do, or many little assignments, planning will help. You'll have time to complete your assignments *and* do the other things you want to do.

This chapter talks about planning ahead to get your assignments done. It also gives you tips for doing the work.

# How to Plan Ahead

- Each day, make a list of the assignments your teacher gives you. (See the next page.)
- Find out what you must do for each assignment.
- Make sure you have everything you need: paper, pens, pencils, your books, your handbook, and so on.
- Plan to work on your assignments at the same time every day.
- Plan to work on a big assignment a little each day.
- Don't rush your assignments!

# Tips for Doing the Work

- **Select a spot.** Study in the same place each day. Pick a quiet place.

- **Follow directions.** If you have a math assignment, make sure to do the right problems!

- **Do the hardest work first.** Do the most difficult work right away, when you have the most energy.

- **Have a reading plan.** When your assignment includes reading, use a reading strategy. (See pages 202-206.)

- **Take breaks.** Take breaks when you really need them. (Not every five minutes, though!)

## Daily Assignment Chart

List the important information for each assignment.

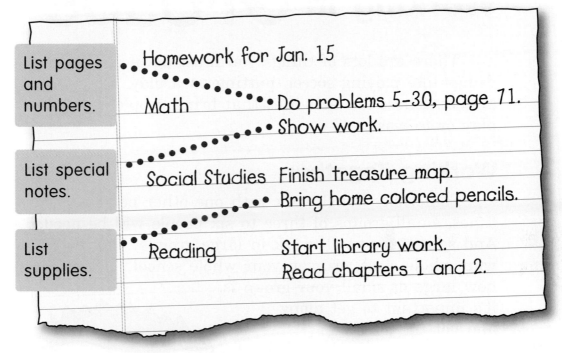

## Weekly Assignment Chart

A chart can help you turn a big assignment into little ones. Here's the first week in a plan for writing an ABC book about nature.

Monday: List words for 10 letters.

Tuesday: List words for other letters. Do research.

Wednesday: Continue research.

Thursday: Begin first draft.

Friday: Continue working on first draft. Begin illustrations.

# Working in Groups

There are lots of things you must do in a group—things like playing soccer, putting on a play, or doing a project. These are activities that bring people together to play or to work.

## Working Together

Sometimes you'll work with one other person. Other times, small groups of three to six people will be needed. And sometimes you'll work in large groups . . . maybe your whole class, or even your whole school. No matter how large or small your group is, it's important to get along and get the job done!

# Working in Pairs

When two people work together, it's called working in pairs. You're partners!

## Tips for Partners

- **Share your ideas.** Talk with each other about what you're going to do. What is your assignment? Writing a poem? Putting on a play?

- **Share jobs.** Decide who will do what. If you're writing a play, for example, each partner could write the lines for different characters.

- **Plan your work.** When is the assignment due? Talk with each other about how much work you will do each day.

- **Listen to each other.** The whole idea of working together is to use two brains instead of one. Offer your ideas, and then listen to your partner's ideas.

# Working in Small Groups

In some ways, working in small groups is like working in pairs. You should all understand the assignment. And everybody should have a chance to talk, while the others listen carefully.

Working in small groups can be harder than working in pairs. There are more people, and sometimes it's tough to agree on things.

# Tips for Group Work

■ **Share and write down ideas.** As group members share their ideas, have someone take notes. This way you'll have a list of everyone's ideas.

> Group Notes
> 1. Wally will bring the treats.
> 2. Jamie said she will pick out the music.

■ **Take turns.** Take turns talking about the different ideas. Say what you like about an idea, and what you don't like. It's okay to disagree in a polite way:

> This idea sounds great, but I don't think we'll have time to do it.

■ **Plan your work.** Combine the best parts of different ideas into one plan that everyone agrees with. For example, if Jon wants to write a play, and Sean wants to write a song, see if you can please both of them:

> Let's write a play that includes a song.

## Making a Plan

Every group project should begin with a plan. The group members should ask themselves these questions:

1. What is our project?
2. When is the project due?
3. What must we do to complete the project?
4. What job (or jobs) will each group member do?

Use an outline like the one below to help your group make its plan. Be sure everyone agrees with the plan.

Group Plan

1. Our project is

2. Our due date is

3. Things we need to do:
   - 
   - 
   - 

4. Jobs for each group member:
   Name:                    Job:
   Name:                    Job:
   Name:                    Job:

# Taking Tests

You may not like taking tests. But you probably don't like eating lumpy oatmeal or going to the dentist, either. So let's forget about what you don't like. Let's be more positive! Tests are a very important part of school. They show how much you've learned about a subject and what you still need to work on.

## Getting Ready

Tests are no problem if you keep up with your class work. It also helps to prepare for each test. In this chapter, you will learn how to study for tests, how to take different types of tests, and more.

# Five Smart Things to Do

**1**

## Listen well.

When your teacher starts talking about your next test, forget about your growling stomach. Listen to everything the teacher tells you about what the test will cover and when it will be given.

**2**

## Gather all of your materials.

Stuff your backpack with everything you need to study, including your textbook and all your notes.

**3**

## Plan your study time.

If your test is two days away, study a little each night before the test. Don't wait until the last minute!

**4**

## Look over everything.

Start with your textbook. Review the chapter page by page. Study the chapter headings and words in bold print. Also look over the review questions at the end of the chapter. Then study your notes or activity sheets. (See page 291 for more ideas.)

**5**

## Find a study partner.

Ask a friend who really wants to study. You could also ask someone in your family.

# Types of Tests

Tests come in many different shapes and sizes. The five most common types are **true/false, matching, multiple choice, fill in the blank,** and **writing prompt.** (You can learn about each type of test on the following pages.)

## True/False Test

On a **true/false test**, you are given a list of sentences. After reading each sentence, you have to decide if it is true or false.

- If any part of the sentence is false, the answer is false. If the whole sentence is true, the answer is true.

- Watch for words like *always, never, all,* or *none.* Sentences using these words are usually false.

**Directions:** Read each sentence carefully. Then put a T before each true statement and an F before each false statement.

_____ 1. New York City has the largest population of any city in the United States.

_____ 2. All major cities are built next to a large body of water.

**Answers:**

1. T

2. F — "All" is the key word that makes this statement false.

## Matching Test

On a **matching test,** you are given two lists of words or phrases. You have to find the ones from each list that go together, or match.

- Before making any matches, read through both lists.

- Put a mark next to each answer you use. Then it will be easier for you to see which answers you have left.

**Directions:** Match the topic in the first column with the correct letter in the second column.

_____ Downtown      a. settled area near a big city

_____ Industrial Region      b. main business district in a city

_____ Suburb      c. area of factories and warehouses

**Answers:**

b. Downtown
c. Industrial Region
a. Suburb

## Multiple-Choice Test

On a **multiple-choice test**, you are given different statements or questions with four or five choices under each one. You must select the best choice to complete the statement or answer the question.

- Read each statement or question very carefully. Look for words like *not, never,* or *except.* They can change the meaning of the statement.

- Study all of the choices. Then select the best one.

**Directions:** Read each statement carefully. Then circle the letter that best completes each one.

1. People move to cities for many reasons, but not for
   (a) jobs   (b) events & activities   (c) peace & quiet

2. City government provides all of the following, except
   (a)  police protection      (c)  street repair
   (b)  grocery stores          (d)  city parks

**Answers:**

1. (c) (People do not move to cities for peace and quiet.)

2. (b) (City governments provide all of the choices, except grocery stores.)

# Fill-in-the-Blank Test

On a **fill-in-the-blank test,** you are given a list of sentences that you must complete. There are no choices given. You must know the right words to fill in the blanks.

- Count the number of blanks to fill in. The number of blanks usually tells you how many words should be in your answer.

- Ask yourself what information fits into the blank. Does the sentence need *a who? a what? a when?* or *a where?*

**Directions:** Carefully read each sentence. Then fill in the blank (or blanks) to complete each statement.

1. In the United States, most people live in _____ areas.

2. _____ and _____ are the two main types of mass transit in a big city.

**Answers:**

1. urban
2. Buses and trains

# Responding to Writing Prompts

On a writing-prompt test, you are asked to respond in writing to a statement or a sentence.

**Sample writing prompt:** Write a paragraph that compares a one-room school to your school.

# Tips for Responding

- **Read the prompt carefully.**

- **Plan your answer.** Because you are asked to compare two things, make two lists—one about a one-room school and one about your school.

| One-Room School | My School |
|---|---|
| kids of different ages | kids close to the same age |
| no janitor | two janitors |
| lunch from home | lunch in cafeteria |

- **Write your answer.** Your first sentence should tell what you are writing about.

A one-room school is not like my school. In a one-room school, kids of all ages are in the same room. In my classroom, the kids are all close to the same age. The kids in one-room schools do chores like sweeping floors and washing blackboards, but two janitors do the chores at my school. We have cafeteria food. The kids in one-room schools bring their lunches from home.

# Remembering for Tests

## Make an idea map.

An idea map will help you organize information you need to remember.

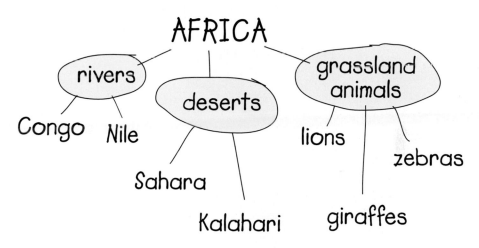

## Use flash cards.

Write one fact on each card. Carry the cards around and read one whenever you have a chance.

## Use a memory trick.

Here's one trick that really works: Let's say you want to remember the names of the five Great Lakes. If you put these names in a certain order, the first letters spell a word.

Huron, Ontario, Michigan, Erie, and Superior spells **HOMES**. (HOMES will help you remember the names of the Great Lakes.)

# Proofreader's Guide

# Marking
# Punctuation

**Punctuation marks** are very important. They help make your ideas clear. Just think what your writing would be like without them. All of your words and ideas would run together.

The first part of the "Proofreader's Guide" gives you the rules for punctuation marks. Turn here when you have questions about punctuation marks.

## On Your Mark

Here's what you'll find in this section:

# Period

A **period** is used at the end of a sentence. A period has other important uses, too.

You've been using periods for years. ←

. . . . . . . . . . . . . . . . . . . . . . . . . . . . . . . . . . . . . . . . . . . . .

| **At the End of a Sentence** | Use a period at the end of a sentence that makes a statement. |
| | We use the computer every day. (statement) |
| | Also use a period at the end of a command. |
| | Please turn off the computer. (command) |

. . . . . . . . . . . . . . . . . . . . . . . . . . . . . . . . . . . . . . . . . . . . .

| **After an Initial** | Use a period after an initial in a person's name. |
| | A. A. Milne   Mary E. Lyons |

. . . . . . . . . . . . . . . . . . . . . . . . . . . . . . . . . . . . . . . . . . . . .

| **After an Abbreviation** | Use a period after an abbreviation that shortens a word. (See page 310.) |
| | Ms.   Mrs.   Mr.   Dr.   W. First St. |

. . . . . . . . . . . . . . . . . . . . . . . . . . . . . . . . . . . . . . . . . . . . .

| **As a Decimal in a Number** | Use a period as a decimal point in numbers. |
| | My mother said my temperature is 99.6 degrees. |
| | Use a period to separate dollars and cents. |
| | It costs $2.50 to see a movie. |

# Comma

**Commas** tell a reader where to rest or pause in a sentence. They are used to make your writing easier to read.

A comma looks like a period with a tail on it (,).

| | |
|---|---|
| **Between Items in a Series** | Use a comma between words or phrases in a series. (A series is a list of three or more things.) |

I like pizza, pickles, and pretzels. (words)

Garfield eats tons of food, talks smart to Jon, and plays tricks on Odie. (phrases)

| | |
|---|---|
| **In Letter Writing** | Use a comma after the greeting in a friendly letter. |

Dear Auntie Liz, (greeting)

Use a comma after the closing in all letters.

Yours truly, (closing)
Sally

| | |
|---|---|
| **To Keep Numbers Clear** | Use a comma in numbers of four or more digits. |

His card collection is worth $1,000.

Our school collected 22,000 soda cans!

# Comma (continued)

| **Between a City and a State** | Use a comma between a city and a state in a sentence or in an address. |
|---|---|

He moved to Sleepy Hollow, New York.
(sentence)

110 Hill Street
Hannibal, MO 63401
(address)

 Do not use a comma between a state and a ZIP code.

| **In Dates and Addresses** | Use a comma between the day and the year in a sentence or in the heading of a letter. |
|---|---|

I saw Uncle Sam on July 4, 2000.
(sentence)

July 4, 2000
(heading of a letter)

 Do not use a comma between a month and a year.

| **In Compound Sentences** | Use a comma before the connecting word in a compound sentence. A compound sentence is made up of two simple sentences that are connected by *or, and,* or *but*. |
|---|---|

I feed Linus, but I don't clean his litter box!

Linus ran away once, and we looked everywhere for him.

## To Set Off a Speaker's Words

Use a comma to set off the exact words of a speaker from the rest of the sentence.

> Maddie said, "If I have four eggs and you have six eggs, what do we get when we put them together?"
> "Ten eggs," said her mother.
> "No," Maddie said, "we get scrambled eggs!"

## After an Introductory Word or Group of Words

### A Word That Shows Surprise

Use a comma to set off an interjection. An interjection is a word that shows surprise.

> Wow, you hit that ball a mile!

### The Name of a Person Spoken To

Use a comma to set off the name of someone you are speaking to.

> Mom, why didn't you come to the game?

### A Group of Words

Use a comma to set off a group of words that comes before the main part of a sentence.

> Because of the storm, Mom missed the game.

## Between Describing Words

Use a comma between two words that describe the same noun.

> His pet is a hairy, black spider!
> I like wearing big, floppy hats.

# Colon

A **colon** is used in three special cases, including to show time.

To make a colon, put one dot on top of another one (:).

| **Between Numbers in Time** | Use a colon between the parts of a number showing time.<br>My school starts at 7:45 a.m.<br>I'll meet you on the playground at 3:30. |

| **In a Business Letter** | Use a colon after the greeting in a business letter.<br>Dear Ms. Yolen:  Dear Editor:<br>Dear Mr. Wilson:  Dear Office Manager: |

| **To Introduce a List** | Use a colon to introduce a list.<br>I don't like to do these things: take showers, do chores, or go to bed early. |

Here are my favorite foods: pizza, spaghetti, and pancakes.

# Apostrophe

An **apostrophe** is used to make contractions or to show ownership.

An apostrophe looks like a *comma*, but it is placed between letters like this:  It's lunchtime!

---

| **In Contractions** | Use an apostrophe to form a contraction. The apostrophe takes the place of one or more letters. |

| Contraction | Short For | Contraction | Short For |
|---|---|---|---|
| don't | do not | they're | they are |
| isn't | is not | you're | you are |
| it's | it is / it has | wasn't | was not |

---

| **To Form Possessives (Ownership)** | **Singular Possessive** An apostrophe plus an *s* is added to a singular noun to show ownership.  (Singular means "one.") |

My friend's dog ate the dish of food. Then it ate the dish!

**Plural Possessive** An apostrophe is usually added after the *s* in a plural noun to show ownership.  (Plural means "more than one.")

The girls' team beat the boys' team.

For plural nouns not ending in *s*, an apostrophe plus an *s* must be added.

My mice's cage is a mess.

# Quotation Marks

**Quotation marks** are used to punctuate titles and to set off a speaker's exact words. Remember that quotation marks always come in pairs. One set comes before the quoted words, and one set comes after them like this:

Porky Pig says, "That's all, folks!"

---

**To Set Off Spoken Words**

Use quotation marks before and after the exact words of the speaker in a sentence.

> "What's that?" I asked.
> My dad said, "It's just a pile of old rags."
> "Dad," I asked, "can rags have a pink nose?"
> Finally, Dad looked carefully into the chicken coop. "It's a possum! We just woke up a sleeping possum."

 **TIP** In almost all cases, punctuation (periods, commas, question marks) is placed inside quotation marks.

---

**To Punctuate Titles**

Use quotation marks to punctuate titles of songs, poems, and short stories.

> We sang "The Lion Sleeps Tonight" in music class.
> Ms. Barr read a poem called "Whispers."
> Lu read a story called "Swamp Monster."

# Hyphen

A **hyphen** is used to divide words. Hyphens can come in handy when you run out of room at the end of a line.

| | |
|---|---|
| **To Divide a Word** | Hawks really like to eat mice, grass-hoppers, and even snakes. A hawk kills a mouse by grabbing it with its claws and shaking it. |
| **T/P** | Divide words only between syllables. (The word *grass-hop-per* can be divided in two places.) |
| **In Fractions** | Use a hyphen between the numbers in fractions written as words.<br>I lost one-half of my allowance! |

# Question Mark

A **question mark** is used at the end of a direct question.

| | |
|---|---|
| **At the End of a Question** | Who put the hot sauce on my taco?<br>Will I ever be able to taste again?<br>Where's the mild sauce? |

# Exclamation Point

An **exclamation point** is used to express strong feeling. It may be placed after a word, a phrase, or a sentence.

**To Express Strong Feeling**

Awesome! ←
(word)

Happy birthday!
(phrase)

There's an alligator!
(sentence)

Don't use too many exclamation points in your writing. They lose their value when they are used again and again.

# Parentheses

**Parentheses** are used to add information. Parentheses always come in pairs.

**To Add Information**

The map (see figure 2) will help you understand the trail.

When you find important information, write down only the main ideas. (This is called note taking.)

# Underlining and Italics

**Underlining** is used to mark titles of books, plays, television programs, movies, and magazines. If you use a computer, you can put titles in *italics* instead of underlining them.

**For Titles**

The Ghostmobile ← underlining
or ← italics
*The Ghostmobile* (a book)

Fantasia or *Fantasia* (a movie)

Nature or *Nature* (a television program)

Cricket or *Cricket* (a magazine)

 **T/P** Use quotation marks (" ") for titles of poems, songs, and short stories.

**For Special Words**

Use underlining (or italics) to mark the names of aircraft and ships.

Merrimac or *Merrimac* (Civil War ship)

Discovery or *Discovery* (spacecraft)

# Checking
# Mechanics

You know all about capitalizing the first word in a sentence. And you know about capitalizing specific names (Abbie, Alabama). But what other words need capital letters? You can find out on the next few pages. Capitalizing words is easy if you know where to look for help.

This section will also help you write plurals of nouns and use numbers and abbreviations correctly. In other words, all of the sticky little problems of **mechanics** are covered here. Your writing will run smoothly if you follow the rules and examples on the next seven pages.

## Mechanic's Tools

Capitalization ▶ **305**

Plurals ▶ **308**

Numbers ▶ **309**

Abbreviations ▶ **310**

# Capitalization

**Proper Nouns and Proper Adjectives**

Capitalize all proper nouns and proper adjectives. A proper noun names a specific person, place, or thing. Proper adjectives are formed from proper nouns.

> Do you know who Rosa Parks is?
> Iowa is a farm state.
> (proper nouns)

> We eat California raisins.

> Where's my Spanish book?
> (proper adjectives)

**Words Used as Nouns**

Capitalize words such as **mother, father, mom, dad, aunt,** and **uncle** when these words are used as names.

> If Dad goes, Uncle Terry will go, too.

No capital letter is needed if you say *our* mother, *my* dad, and so on.

> My dad asked me to go to the mall.

**Titles Used with Names**

Capitalize titles used with names.

> President Abraham Lincoln
> Mr. Ramirez
> Dr. Martin Luther King, Jr.
> Mayor Barbara Long

Do not capitalize titles when they are used alone: the **president,** the **doctor,** the **mayor.**

# Capitalization (continued)

| **Abbreviations** | Capitalize abbreviations of titles and organizations. |
| --- | --- |

> Mr. (Mister)
> ABC (American Broadcasting Company)
> NFL (National Football League)

| **Titles** | Capitalize the first word of a title, the last word, and every important word in between. |
| --- | --- |

> "When You Wish upon a Star" (song)
> Beauty and the Beast (movie)
> The Enormous Egg (book)

| **First Words** | Capitalize the first word of every sentence. |
| --- | --- |

> The first day at school is exciting.

Capitalize the first word of a direct quotation.

> Mr. Hon said, "Welcome to my class."

| **Days and Months** | Capitalize the names of days of the week, months of the year, and special holidays. |
| --- | --- |

> Friday    April    Fourth of July
> Thanksgiving    Arbor Day

**TIP** Do not capitalize the seasons: *winter, spring, summer, fall.*

## Geographic Names

Planets and heavenly bodies .................**Earth, Mars, Milky Way**

Continents.........................**Europe, Asia, Africa, North America**

Countries ...............**Canada, Mexico, United States of America**

States .........................**Utah, Ohio, Washington, Maine, Indiana**

Provinces........................**Nova Scotia, Quebec, Newfoundland**

Cities and counties ..................................**Buffalo, New York City, Mexico City, Los Angeles County**

Bodies of water ......................................**Red Sea, Lake Michigan, Mississippi River, Atlantic Ocean, Gulf of Mexico, St. Lawrence Seaway**

Landforms..............................................**Rocky Mountains, Mount Everest, Hawaiian Islands**

Public areas...........................................**Statue of Liberty Island, Yellowstone National Park**

Streets, roads, and highways.................**Santa Monica Freeway, Main Street, Rock Road, Skyline Drive, Park Avenue, Interstate 95**

Buildings .......................................**Sears Tower, Lincoln Center, Petronas Towers**

| Capitalize | Do Not Capitalize |
| --- | --- |
| **January, October** ........................ | spring, summer, winter, fall |
| **Mother** (as a name) ................. | my **mother** (describing her) |
| **President** Washington............................ | our first **president** |
| **Mayor** Hefty ........................................ | Ms. Hefty, our **mayor** |
| **Lake** Erie ......................................................... | the **lake** area |
| the **South** (section of the country) .......... | **south** (a direction) |
| planet **Earth** ............................................. | the **earth** we live on |

# Plurals

| **Most Nouns** | Plurals of most nouns are made by adding an *s*.<br><br>balloon ➜ balloons    shoe ➜ shoes |
|---|---|

| **Nouns Ending in sh, ch, x, s, and z** | The plurals of nouns ending in **sh, ch, x, s,** and **z** are made by adding **es** to the singular.<br><br>wish ➜ wishes      lunch ➜ lunches<br>box ➜ boxes       buzz ➜ buzzes<br>dress ➜ dresses |
|---|---|

| **Nouns Ending in y** | The plurals of nouns that end in **y** (with a consonant letter just before the **y**) are formed by changing the **y** to **i** and adding **es**.<br><br>sky ➜ skies      story ➜ stories<br>puppy ➜ puppies      city ➜ cities<br><br>The plurals of nouns that end in **y** (with a vowel before the **y**) are formed by adding **s**.<br><br>monkey ➜ monkeys      day ➜ days<br>toy ➜ toys        key ➜ keys |
|---|---|

| **Irregular Nouns** | Some nouns form a plural by taking on an irregular spelling.<br><br>child ➜ children<br>mouse ➜ mice<br>goose ➜ geese |
|---|---|

# Numbers

| **Writing Numbers** | Numbers from one to nine are usually written as words; all numbers 10 and over are usually written as numerals. |

one   four   23   45   365   5,280

**Except:** Numbers being compared should be kept in the same style.

> Students from 6 to 10 years old are in the choir.

| **Very Large Numbers** | You may use a combination of numbers and words for very large numbers. |

17 million          1.5 billion

| **Sentence Beginnings** | Use words, not numerals, to begin a sentence. |

> Eleven students in the class had brown hair.

| **Numerals Only** | Use numerals for any numbers in the following forms: |

**money** ...................... $1.50          **decimals** ...................... 98.6

**percentages** ...... 50 percent          **pages** ........... pages 12-21

**chapters** ........... chapter 5          **addresses** ........ 701 Hill St.

**dates** ..................... June 6          **times** ................. 3:30 p.m.

**statistics** ..................................................... a score of 5 to 2

# Abbreviations

**Common Abbreviations**

An **abbreviation** is the shortened form of a word or phrase. Many abbreviations begin with a capital letter and end with a period.

Mrs.    Mr.    Dr.    Ave.
a.m.    p.m.    adj. (adjective)

**Days of the Week**

| | | | |
|---|---|---|---|
| Sun. | (Sunday) | Thurs. | (Thursday) |
| Mon. | (Monday) | Fri. | (Friday) |
| Tues. | (Tuesday) | Sat. | (Saturday) |
| Wed. | (Wednesday) | | |

**Months of the Year**

| | | | |
|---|---|---|---|
| Jan. | (January) | Jul. | (July) |
| Feb. | (February) | Aug. | (August) |
| Mar. | (March) | Sept. | (September) |
| Apr. | (April) | Oct. | (October) |
| May | (May) | Nov. | (November) |
| Jun. | (June) | Dec. | (December) |

**Acronyms**

An **acronym** is a word formed from the first letter or letters of words in a phrase.

SADD (**S**tudents **A**gainst **D**estructive **D**ecisions)

**Initialisms**

An **initialism** is like an acronym, but the initials (letters) are not pronounced as a word.

CD (**c**ompact **d**isc)    TV (**t**ele**v**ision)

## State Abbreviations

| | Standard | Postal | | Standard | Postal |
|---|---|---|---|---|---|
| Alabama | Ala. | **AL** | Missouri | Mo. | **MO** |
| Alaska | Alaska | **AK** | Montana | Mont. | **MT** |
| Arizona | Ariz. | **AZ** | Nebraska | Neb. | **NE** |
| Arkansas | Ark. | **AR** | Nevada | Nev. | **NV** |
| California | Calif. | **CA** | New Hampshire | N.H. | **NH** |
| Colorado | Colo. | **CO** | New Jersey | N.J. | **NJ** |
| Connecticut | Conn. | **CT** | New Mexico | N.M. | **NM** |
| Delaware | Del. | **DE** | New York | N.Y. | **NY** |
| District of | | | North Carolina | N.C. | **NC** |
| Columbia | D.C. | **DC** | North Dakota | N.D. | **ND** |
| Florida | Fla. | **FL** | Ohio | Ohio | **OH** |
| Georgia | Ga. | **GA** | Oklahoma | Okla. | **OK** |
| Hawaii | Hawaii | **HI** | Oregon | Ore. | **OR** |
| Idaho | Idaho | **ID** | Pennsylvania | Pa. | **PA** |
| Illinois | Ill. | **IL** | Rhode Island | R.I. | **RI** |
| Indiana | Ind. | **IN** | South Carolina | S.C. | **SC** |
| Iowa | Iowa | **IA** | South Dakota | S.D. | **SD** |
| Kansas | Kan. | **KS** | Tennessee | Tenn. | **TN** |
| Kentucky | Ky. | **KY** | Texas | Tex. | **TX** |
| Louisiana | La. | **LA** | Utah | Utah | **UT** |
| Maine | Maine | **ME** | Vermont | Vt. | **VT** |
| Maryland | Md. | **MD** | Virginia | Va. | **VA** |
| Massachusetts | Mass. | **MA** | Washington | Wash. | **WA** |
| Michigan | Mich. | **MI** | West Virginia | W. Va. | **WV** |
| Minnesota | Minn. | **MN** | Wisconsin | Wis. | **WI** |
| Mississippi | Miss. | **MS** | Wyoming | Wyo. | **WY** |

## Address Abbreviations

| | | | | | |
|---|---|---|---|---|---|
| Avenue | Ave. | **AVE** | North | N. | **N** |
| Boulevard | Blvd. | **BLVD** | Road | Rd. | **RD** |
| Court | Ct. | **CT** | South | S. | **S** |
| Drive | Dr. | **DR** | Square | Sq. | **SQ** |
| East | E. | **E** | Street | St. | **ST** |
| Highway | Hwy. | **HWY** | West | W. | **W** |

 Use postal abbreviations when addressing envelopes.

# Checking Your
# Spelling

The spelling words are listed in alphabetical (ABC) order by their first letter, then by each following letter. For example, in the "A" column, the words **almost, alone,** and **always** begin with **al.** For these three words, you must look at the third letter to see their alphabetical order.

Use this spelling list when you proofread your writing.

## A

about
afraid
after
again
almost
alone
always
angry
animal
another
answer
anybody
April
aren't
asked
asleep
August
aunt
author

## B

bear
beautiful
because
behind
believe
better
blood
body
both
bought
break
breakfast
bright
built
bunch
bushes

## C

captain
care
catch
caught
cause
change
cheese
children
climb
clothes
could
country
cousin
cover
crazy

## D

dance
daughter
dead
dear
December
decided
desk
didn't
different
dirty
doesn't
dressed
drive
dropped
dumb
during

## E

early
earth
either
engine
enough
everyone
everything

## F

famous
favorite
February
few
field

fight
finally
finger
finished
first
flew
floor
flying
folks
follow
forest
forget
forgive
fought
Friday
front

## G

ghost
giant
grade
ground
group
guess
gym

## H

half
happen
happiness
heard
heart
hello
high

honey
hospital
huge
hungry
hurry
hurt

## I

idea
I'll
I'm
important
inches
inside
instead
interest
island
isn't
it's

## J

jail
January
join
July
June

## K

kept
kitchen
knew
knife
knocked
know

## L

laugh
learn
leave
library
listen
loose
loud
lunch

## M

machine
mail
March
May
maybe
metal
middle
might
minute
mirror
Monday
monster
mouse
mouth
movie
music

## N

near
neighbor
nobody
noise

north
nothing
November

## O

ocean
o'clock
October
often
once
orange
other
outside
own

## P

paint
paper
parents
past
pencil
people
person
phone
picture
piece
planet
pleased
police
poor
power
president
pretty
probably

**Q**

question
quick
quiet

**R**

reached
ready
really
reason
remember
report
rest
right
river
rocket
rough
round

**S**

Saturday
scared
science
scream
secret
September
sight
since
small
someone
something
special
spring

stairs
strange
strong
Sunday
sure
surprise

**T**

taught
their
thought
threw
through
Thursday
together
tonight
toward
trouble
truth
Tuesday

**U**

uncle
understand
until
upon
usual

**V**

visit
voice

**W**

wasn't
watch
wear
weather
Wednesday
which
whole
window
winter
without
woman
women
word
world
worry
would
wrong

**X**

X ray
xylophone

**Y**

young
you're

**Z**

zero

# Using the
# Right Word

This section lists common homophones. Homophones are words that sound the same but have different spellings and meanings, like **to, too,** and **two.** If you know the common homophones, you would write this:

> I blew my nose.
> *not*
> I blue my nose.

| | |
|---|---|
| **ant,**<br>**aunt** | An ant is an insect that works hard.<br>It's a blast when my aunt baby-sits for us. |
| **ate,**<br>**eight** | I ate the teacher's apple.<br>My friend had eight pieces of licorice. |
| **bare,**<br>**bear** | She tested the water with her bare feet.<br>The bear ate the berries. |

| | |
|---|---|
| **blew, blue** | We blew bubbles at the parade.<br>The ocean is blue because of the sky. |
| **brake, break** | His bicycle has a bad brake.<br>It will break if he presses on it too hard. |
| **buy, by** | I need to buy a new lamp.<br>Did that light go on all by itself? |
| **cent, scent, sent** | I bought a green birthday candle for one cent.<br>The candle has a pine scent.<br>He sent her a birthday card. |
| **close, clothes** | Close the door.<br>Put the clothes in the dryer. |
| **creak, creek** | Old boats creak when they move.<br>The water in the creek smells funny. |
| **dear, deer** | Jasmine is my dear friend.<br>Deer come out of the woods to feed. |
| **dew, do, due** | You'll find dew on the grass in the morning.<br>I do my homework right away.<br>My report is due today. |
| **eye, I** | Sam wore an eye patch to look like a pirate.<br>I played the part of the captain. |
| **for, four** | I like popcorn for a snack.<br>My four brothers love chips and salsa. |

| | |
|---|---|
| **hare, hair** | **A hare looks like a large rabbit.** <br> **My hair sometimes looks like a wet rabbit.** |
| **heal, heel** | **It takes about a week for a cut to heal.** <br> **The heel of my shoe came off!** |
| **hear, here** | **I can't hear you.** <br> **I was right here all of the time.** |
| **heard, herd** | **I heard the noise from the street.** <br> **It sounded like a herd of buffalo!** |
| **hole, whole** | **My basketball has a hole in it.** <br> **That ruined my whole day.** |
| **hour, our** | **The assembly lasted one hour.** <br> **Our class sat in the front row.** |
| **its, it's** | **Our class needs its sharpener fixed.** <br> (*Its* shows ownership.) <br> **It's eating all our pencils.** <br> (It's = It is) |
| **knew, new** | **I knew everyone's name on the first day.** <br> **Vanessa is a new girl in my class.** |
| **knight, night** | **The knight put on his armor.** <br> **He can't go out at night.** |
| **know, no** | **Do you know how this thing works?** <br> **No, I'll have to ask my teacher.** |

| | |
|---|---|
| **made, maid** | Who made this mess? <br> Cinderella was a maid. |
| **main, mane** | My main skill is fly catching. <br> The horse's mane needs brushing. |
| **meat, meet** | My older sister doesn't eat meat. <br> I will meet her at the health-food store. |
| **one, won** | The pitcher threw one ball and two strikes. <br> They won the game in the last inning. |
| **pair, pare, pear** | The pair of shoes had orange laces. <br> Machines can pare apples in 10 seconds. <br> A pear is a fruit a little bit like an apple. |
| **peace, piece** | Who likes peace and quiet? <br> Alex got the biggest piece of cake. |
| **plain, plane** | Grandma likes plain toast for breakfast. <br> Buffalo eat the long grass on the plain. <br> The stunt plane flew upside down. |
| **read, red** | Have you read any books by Jane Yolen? <br> Why do you always eat the red jelly beans? |
| **right, write** | He must have said turn right! <br> Next time, I'll write down the directions. |
| **road, rode, rowed** | I saw a covered bridge on a country road. <br> My sister rode my bike all day. <br> We rowed the boat to the island. |

| | |
|---|---|
| **scene, seen** | The movie has a great mountain scene. Have you seen mountains before? |
| **sea, see** | A sea is like an ocean. I can't see anything in the dark. |
| **sew, so, sow** | My brother had to sew the sail. Get in so we can get going! Each spring we sow seeds in our garden. |
| **soar, sore** | Hawks soar high in the air. One hawk had a sore wing. |
| **some, sum** | I have some good news and some bad news. The sum of two numbers is the total. |
| **son, sun** | My grandpa is the son of a baker. The sun is only 93 million miles from us. |
| **tail, tale** | The monkey liked to swing by its tail. My teacher told a tall tale about Pecos Bill. |
| **their, there, they're** | The girls won their soccer game. (*Their* shows ownership.) There are 12 girls on the team. Now they're the champs. (they're = they are) |
| **threw, through** | The pitcher threw a fastball. It went right through the strike zone. |

| | |
|---|---|
| **to,** <br> **two,** <br> **too** | **We went to the zoo.** <br> **We took two buses.** <br> **Daryl ate too much food.** <br> (*Too* means "more than enough" or "very.") <br> **I ate a lot of food, too.** <br> (*Too* means "also.") |
| **waist,** <br> **waste** | **She wore a yellow belt around her waist.** <br> **Don't waste paper!** |
| **wait,** <br> **weight** | **We had to wait 20 minutes.** <br> **Our dog has to lose weight.** |
| **way,** <br> **weigh** | **Am I going the right way?** <br> **I want to weigh my cat.** |
| **weak,** <br> **week** | **My skinny arms are weak.** <br> **Next week I'll start exercising.** |
| **wear,** <br> **where** | **Which baseball cap should I wear?** <br> **Where are you going?** |
| **which,** <br> **witch** | **Which book should I read?** <br> **I like The Lion, the Witch, and the Wardrobe.** |
| **wood,** <br> **would** | **The doghouse was made of wood.** <br> **Would Mugsy like it?** |
| **your,** <br> **you're** | **Pick up your clothes before Mom gets home.** <br> (*Your* shows ownership.) <br> **You're right about my room.** <br> (You're = You are) |

# Understanding
# Sentences

## Important Things to Know About Sentences

**1** A sentence is a complete thought.

**2** A sentence has two basic parts—a subject and a predicate (verb).

**3** A sentence makes a statement, asks a question, gives a command, or shows strong emotion.

**4** A sentence begins with a capital letter and ends with a period, a question mark, or an exclamation point.

You can find more about sentences on the next three pages and on pages 71-73.

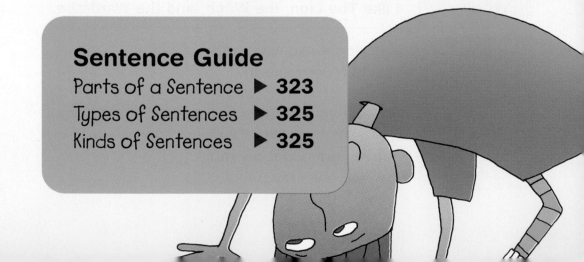

## Sentence Guide

# Parts of a Sentence

**Subject**

The **subject** names someone or something. The subject is often doing something.

> The huge balloon is full of water.
> (**The huge balloon** is the complete subject.)

> My big sister threw the balloon.
> (**My big sister** is the complete subject.)

> My best friend caught the balloon.
> (**My best friend** is the complete subject.)

**Simple Subject**

The **simple subject** is the main word in the subject.

> The huge balloon is full of water.
> (**Balloon** is the simple subject.)

> My big sister threw the balloon.
> (**Sister** is the simple subject.)

> My best friend caught the balloon.
> (**Friend** is the simple subject.)

**Compound Subject**

A **compound subject** is made up of two or more simple subjects joined by **and** or **or**.

> My big sister and my best friend played catch with the balloon.
> (**Sister** and **friend** make up the compound subject.)

**Predicate (Verb)**

The **predicate** tells what the subject is or does.

> Rocky is the fastest dog on the block.
> (**Is the fastest dog on the block** is the complete predicate.)

> Rocky runs faster than the other dogs.
> (**Runs faster than the other dogs** is the complete predicate.)

**Simple Predicate (Verb)**

The **simple predicate** is the main word in the predicate part of the sentence.

> Rocky is the fastest dog on the block.
> (**Is** is the simple predicate.)

> Rocky runs faster than the other dogs.
> (**Runs** is the simple predicate.)

**Compound Predicate (Verb)**

A **compound predicate** has two or more simple predicates (verbs) joined by *and* or *or.*

> Rocky runs fast and barks loud.
> (**Runs** and **barks** make up the compound predicate.)

**Subject-Verb Agreement**

The **subject and verb** of a sentence must "agree" with one another.

> My dog likes treats. (The singular subject **dog** agrees with the verb **likes**.)

> My dogs like treats. (The plural subject **dogs** agrees with the verb **like**.)

# Types of Sentences

| Simple Sentence | A **simple sentence** has a complete idea. |

Gloria sings.
(This is a simple sentence.)
Gloria and Matt sing.
(This sentence has two simple subjects.)
Gloria sings and dances.
(This sentence has two simple predicates.)

**Compound Sentence**

A **compound sentence** is two simple sentences joined by a comma and connecting word *(and, but, or)*.

Twila played drums, and she sang.

# Kinds of Sentences

**Declarative Sentence**

A **declarative** sentence makes a statement.

The capital of Wisconsin is Madison.

**Interrogative Sentence**

An **interrogative** sentence asks a question.

What is the capital of Oregon?

**Imperative Sentence**

An **imperative** sentence gives a command or makes a request.

Write the capital of your state.

**Exclamatory Sentence**

An **exclamatory** sentence shows strong emotion or surprise.

Cleveland is not the capital of Ohio!

# Understanding Our
# Language

All the words in our language fit into eight groups.
These word groups are called the **parts of speech**.

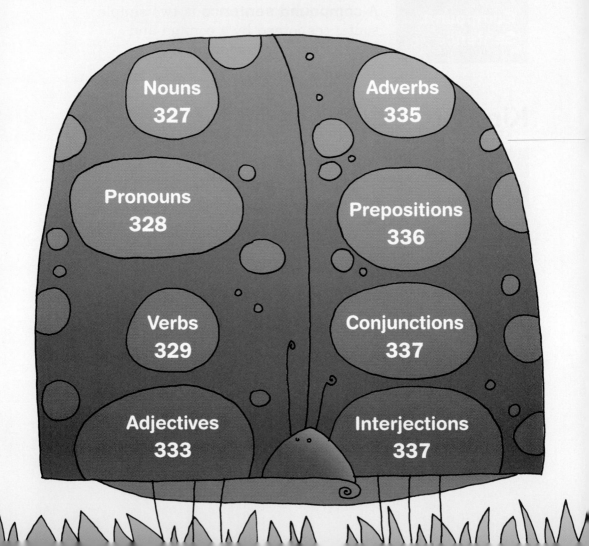

Nouns
327

Adverbs
335

Pronouns
328

Prepositions
336

Verbs
329

Conjunctions
337

Adjectives
333

Interjections
337

# Nouns

A **noun** names a person, a place, a thing, or an idea.

runner    Los Angeles    race    joy

# Kinds of Nouns

| | |
|---|---|
| **Common Nouns** | A **common noun** names any person, place, thing, or idea.<br><br>girl    building    team |
| **Proper Nouns** | A **proper noun** names a specific person, place, thing, or idea. Proper nouns are capitalized.<br><br>Ann    Sears Tower    Atlanta Braves |
| **Singular Nouns** | A **singular noun** names one person, place, thing, or idea.<br><br>kid    bus    can |
| **Plural Nouns** | A **plural noun** names more than one person, place, thing, or idea.<br><br>kids    buses    cans |
| **Possessive Nouns** | A **possessive noun** shows ownership.<br><br>My school's colors are blue and white. (Add 's after a singular noun.)<br><br>Both schools' teams played well. (Add only ' after most plural nouns.) |

# Pronouns

A **pronoun** is a word that takes the place of a noun.

Karl climbed over the fence.

He could have been hurt.
(The pronoun *he* replaces the noun *Karl.*)

The lunchroom was a busy place.

It was very crowded.
(The pronoun *it* replaces the noun *lunchroom.*)

## Kinds of Pronouns

**Possessive Pronouns**

A **possessive pronoun** shows ownership.

Karl hurt his arm while climbing the fence.
(Karl's arm)

Our lunch table was messy.

Kendra left her lunch on the table.
(Kendra's lunch)

**Common Personal Pronouns**

**Singular Pronouns**

I, me, my, mine,
you, your, yours,
he, him, his,
she, her, hers,
it, its

**Plural Pronouns**

we, us, our, ours,
you, your, yours,
they, them, their,
theirs

Today's
Lunch
- pizza pockets
- carrot

# Verbs

A **verb** shows action or links two ideas in a sentence.

The monkey swings through the branches.

I am happy.

## Types of Verbs

| **Action Verbs** | An **action verb** tells what the subject is doing. |
|---|---|

> I raced the dog.
>
> Todd jumped like a kangaroo.

| **Linking Verbs** | A **linking verb** links the subject to a word in the predicate part of a sentence. (The predicate tells what the subject is or does.) |
|---|---|

> My teacher is helpful.
> (The verb *is* links **teacher** to **helpful.**)
>
> My friends are happy in our school.
> (The verb *are* links **friends** to **happy.**)

**Linking Verbs:** is, are, was, were, am, be, been

| **Helping Verbs** | A **helping verb** comes before the main verb, and it helps state an action or show time. |
|---|---|

> Pat has called two times.
> (*Has* helps the main action verb *called.*)
>
> Pat will be here tomorrow.
> (*Will* helps the main linking verb *be.*)

**Helping Verbs:** has, have, had, will, could, should, would, do, did, may, can

# Tenses of Verbs

The **tense** of a verb tells when the action takes place. Tense is often shown by endings (play**s**, play**ed**) and by helping verbs (**will** play, **has** play**ed**).

| | |
|---|---|
| **Present Tense Verbs** | **Present tense** means the action is happening now or that it happens all of the time. |

Jackie plays on our soccer team.

Our practices help us a lot.

• • • • • • • • • • • • • • • • • • • • • • • • • • • • • • • • • • • • • •

| | |
|---|---|
| **Past Tense Verbs** | **Past tense** means the action happened before, or in the past. |

Yesterday Jackie played forward.

Three girls scored goals.

• • • • • • • • • • • • • • • • • • • • • • • • • • • • • • • • • • • • • •

| | |
|---|---|
| **Future Tense Verbs** | **Future tense** means the action will take place at a later time, or in the future. |

Tomorrow Jackie will play goalie.

We will see a soccer video.

**TIP** Some verbs tell the time of the action in other ways.

Jackie has played soccer for three years.

Our coach is planning a tournament.

The soccer field had been a pasture.

# Forms of Verbs

| **Singular Verbs** | The verb in a sentence must agree, or make sense, with the subject. Use a **singular verb** when the subject is singular. Remember that *singular* means "one." |

> Kayla eats powdered donuts.
> (**Eats** is a singular verb.)
>
> She gets powder all over her mouth.
> (**Gets** is a singular verb.)

| **Plural Verbs** | Use a **plural verb** when the subject is plural. Remember that *plural* means "more than one." |

> The other girls love chocolate donuts.
> (**Love** is a plural verb.)
>
> They save the frosting part for last.
> (**Save** is a plural verb.)

| **Regular Verbs** | Many verbs in our language are **regular**. Add *ed* to regular verbs to form the past tense. |

> I play.    Yesterday I played.
> He kicks.    He has kicked.

| **Irregular Verbs** | Some verbs in our language are **irregular**. (See the next page for a chart.) |

> I see.    I saw.    I have seen.
> She writes. She wrote. She has written.

**T/P** The most common irregular verb is the verb *be*. Different forms of the verb include *am, is, are, was, were,* and *been.*

# Common Irregular Verbs

| Present Tense | Past Tense | Past Tense with *has, have, had* |
|---|---|---|
| am, are | was, were | been |
| begin | began | begun |
| break | broke | broken |
| catch | caught | caught |
| come | came | come |
| do | did | done |
| draw | drew | drawn |
| drive | drove | driven |
| eat | ate | eaten |
| fall | fell | fallen |
| fly | flew | flown |
| freeze | froze | frozen |
| give | gave | given |
| go | went | gone |
| grow | grew | grown |
| hide | hid | hidden, hid |
| know | knew | known |
| ride | rode | ridden |
| ring | rang | rung |
| run | ran | run |
| see | saw | seen |
| sing | sang, sung | sung |
| speak | spoke | spoken |
| take | took | taken |
| throw | threw | thrown |
| write | wrote | written |

# Adjectives

An **adjective** is a word that describes a noun or a pronoun. Adjectives tell *what kind, how many,* or *which one.*

Some dogs have funny faces.
(An adjective usually comes before the word it describes.)

The fur on a sheepdog is fluffy.
(An adjective may come after a linking verb like **is** or **are**.)

| **Articles** | The articles *a, an,* and *the* are adjectives. |

A pug is a small dog.
(**A** is used before words beginning with a consonant sound.)

An Airedale is a large terrier.
(**An** is used before words beginning with a vowel sound.)

# Kinds of Adjectives

| **Proper Adjectives** | Some adjectives are formed from proper nouns. They are always capitalized. |

The dingo is an Australian dog.

| **Compound Adjectives** | Some adjectives are made up of more than one word. Some are spelled as one word, and some are hyphenated. |

A dalmatian has a shorthaired coat.

A dachshund has a sausage-shaped body.

# Forms of Adjectives

**Positive Adjectives**

An adjective describes a person, place, or thing.

A bloodhound has a wrinkled face.

**Comparative Adjectives**

Some **adjectives** compare two people, places, or things.

A bulldog is smaller than a dalmatian. (Many comparative adjectives use the ending *er*.)

Bulldogs are more muscular than poodles. (The word *more* is used before some adjectives with two or more syllables.)

**Superlative Adjectives**

Some adjectives compare three or more people, places, or things.

That Chihuahua is the smallest dog I have ever seen. (Many superlative adjectives use the ending *est*.)

The golden retriever is one of the most beautiful dogs. (The word *most* is used before some adjectives with two or more syllables.)

**Irregular Forms of Adjectives**

The adjectives in this chart use different words to make comparisons.

| Positive | Comparative | Superlative |
| --- | --- | --- |
| good | better | best |
| bad | worse | worst |
| many | more | most |

# Adverbs

An **adverb** is a word that describes a verb. It tells how or when an action is done.

The desert temperature rises quickly.

Desert animals hunt for food nightly.

 Adverbs often end with **ly,** but not always. Words like **not, never, very,** and **always** are common adverbs.

# Kinds of Adverbs

| | |
|---|---|
| **Adverbs of Time (When)** | Some adverbs tell **how often** or **when** an action is done.<br><br>Sand dunes often change their shape.<br><br>A group of scientists explored the desert yesterday. |
| **Adverbs of Place (Where)** | Some adverbs tell **where** something happens.<br><br>One scientist worked nearby.<br><br>She stayed outside for a long time. |
| **Adverbs of Manner (How)** | Adverbs often tell **how** something is done.<br><br>The desert sun shone brightly.<br><br>The horned viper moved silently. |

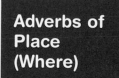

# Prepositions

A **preposition** is a word that introduces a prepositional phrase.

> Todd slept under the covers. (**Under** is a preposition.)

> Teddy slept on the chair. (**On** is a preposition.)

| Prepositional Phrases | A prepositional phrase begins with a preposition, and it ends with a noun or a pronoun. |
| --- | --- |

> Todd has a stuffed animal under his arm.

> Teddy sleeps on his side.

## Common Prepositions

| | | | | |
| --- | --- | --- | --- | --- |
| about | during | onto | through | until |
| above | for | out of | to | up |
| across | from | outside | toward | with |
| after | in | over | under | within |
| against | inside | past | underneath | without |
| along | into | since | | |
| among | like | | | |
| around | near | | | |
| at | of | | | |
| before | off | | | |
| behind | on | | | |
| below | | | | |
| beneath | | | | |
| between | | | | |
| by | | | | |

on

inside

under

near

# Conjunctions

A **conjunction** connects words or groups of words.

| **Coordinating Conjunctions** | The most common conjunctions are listed here. They are called **coordinating conjunctions.** |

    and  but  or  nor  for  so  yet

We could use skateboards or bikes.
(**Or** connects two words.)

Maya wrote a poem and sang a song.
(**And** connects two phrases.)

We ate breakfast early, but we still missed the bus.
(**But** connects two simple sentences.)

| **Other Conjunctions** | Other conjunctions help you connect ideas in very specific ways. Here are some of these conjunctions: |

| after | before | until | where |
| because | since | when | while |

I like to skateboard when it is hot.
She likes to fish after it rains.

# Interjections

An **interjection** is a word or phrase used to express strong emotion or surprise. It is followed by an exclamation point or by a comma.

Hey! Slow down!    Wow, look at him go!

# Student Almanac

Using Language

Exploring Science

Improving Math Skills

Using Maps

History in the Making

# Using Language

The **English** language is related to other languages, just like we are related to other people. In some ways, we look or sound like our parents and grandparents. English looks and sounds like its relatives, too. The closest language relatives—especially German and French—have helped make English what it is today. There's lots to learn about the history of the English language and about how to use it properly.

In this section of the "Almanac," you'll learn the history of our language, how to use sign language, and even how to improve your personal handwriting.

# History of the English Language

The story of the English language really began more than 2,000 years ago with a tribe of people in Britain called the Celts. The Romans invaded Britain in 43 C.E. They stayed for a while and left behind roads, buildings, and, most importantly, the Roman alphabet. This is the same alphabet English speakers use today!

About 500 years later, three German tribes—the Angles, Saxons, and Jutes—crossed the North Sea to invade Britain. They brought a lot of German words. They pushed the Celts out of the way, but mixed the languages together. Since the Angle tribe was the biggest, the country became known as Angleland, or England.

In 1066, the Normans invaded England from France. The Normans spoke French. As they lived in England, they began to use English; but they also used some French words like *hotel* and *nation* to help them feel more at home.

## English in the Middle Ages

Some of the first readers and writers in England were priests and scholars. They liked to use Greek and Latin. As English became more popular, they added some Greek and Latin words to the language.

At this time, people in different places spoke English differently. The invention of printed books in the 1400s changed that. Most books were printed in London. As people read more, they learned London English. Before long, many people were using the same kind of English.

## English in America

When English people came to North America, they brought their language. The Native Americans, who were already here, added more words to English. They added words like *moccasin, raccoon*, and *skunk*. Native people from Central America added words like *tomato, chocolate,* and *hurricane*. Later, the Spanish-speaking people who came to America added words like *ranch* and *alligator*.

## New Words

New inventions and new ways of thinking have also added words to our language. Over time, *telephone, software*, and *Internet* have become part of the language.

Today, English is a language of about 500,000 words. And, of course, our language will continue to grow as the world changes.

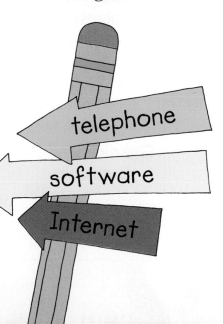

# English from Around the World

Words from many languages have been added to English. This chart shows you some of these words.

**Old English**
man, woman
morning, night
day, month, year
cat, dog, house
red, yellow
at, in, by, from
cow, calf, pig

**Scandinavian**
they, them, their
knife, sky, ski
happy, scare, egg

**French**
constitution, city
state, nation
congress, mayor
poetry, art
court, medicine
dance, fashion
tailor, physician
beef, veal, pork

**Greek**
paragraph
school
alphabet
stomach

**Latin**
camp, wine
paper, perfume
umbrella, mile
senator
legislator

**Native American**
canoe
toboggan
opossum
moose
chipmunk
pecan, hickory
igloo, kayak

**Spanish**
cigar, mosquito
tornado
rodeo, canyon

**Italian**
spaghetti, pizza
macaroni
balcony, bank
piano, balloon
tarantula
volcano

**Dutch**
cookie
coleslaw
deck, dock
boss, pump

**German**
hamburger
kindergarten
pretzel, book

**Asian**
pepper, panther
shampoo, silk
tea, jungle
ketchup

**Australian**
kangaroo

**African**
chimpanzee
banana
banjo, okra

**Middle Eastern**
candy, cotton
coffee, sugar
spinach, tiger

# Saying Hello and Good-Bye

There are more than 220 languages in the world today. No wonder people sometimes have trouble speaking to each other, especially when they travel! Here are some "hello" and "good-bye" words that make things a little easier.

| Language | Hello or Good Day | Good-Bye |
|---|---|---|
| Chinese (Mandarin dialect) | dzău | dzàijyàn |
| French | bonjour | au revoir |
| German | guten Tag | auf Wiedersehen |
| Hebrew | shalom | shalom |
| Italian | buon giorno | addio |
| Farsi (Iran) | salaam  | khoda hafez خدا حافظ |
| Portuguese | alô | adeus |
| Swahili | neno la kusalimu rafiki au mtani | kwa heri |
| Spanish | hola | adiós |
| Swedish | god dag | adjö |

**On Track** The words for saying "hello" and "good-bye" in different languages may look or sound alike. Many languages of today began as the same language thousands of years ago. That's why many words are similar.

# Using Sign Language
## Manual Alphabet

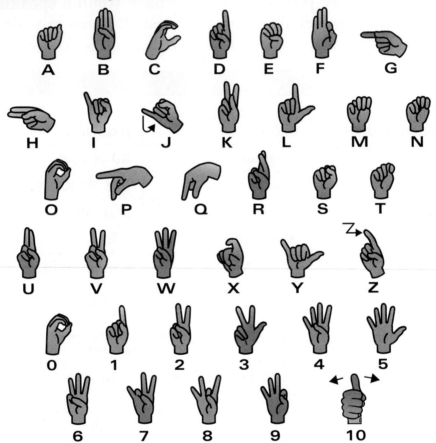

# Braille Alphabet and Numbers

# Improving Your Handwriting
## Manuscript Alphabet

A B C D E
F G H I J K
L M N O P
Q R S T U V
W X Y Z

a b c d e f g h i
j k l m n o p q r
s t u v w x y z

## Continuous Stroke Alphabet

A B C D E

F G H I J K

L M N O P

Q R S T U V

W X Y Z

a b c d e f g h i

j k l m n o p q r

s t u v w x y z

## Cursive Alphabet

*Aa Bb Cc Dd Ee*
*Ff Gg Hh Ii*
*Jj Kk Ll Mm*
*Nn Oo Pp Qq Rr*
*Ss Tt Uu Vv*
*Ww Xx Yy Zz*

# Handwriting Checklist

___ Do I sit up straight and slant my paper?

___ Do I hold my pencil correctly?

___ Are all of my letters formed correctly?

___ Do all of my letters slant the same way?

___ Are my letters too close or too far apart?

___ Do I have the right amount of space between each word?

___ Does my final draft look neat?

# Exploring Science

Exploring science will take you on a journey to discover some of the wonders of life. On this journey, you can study about living things, like animals, and nonliving things, like planets.

The charts and lists in this chapter will give you facts about some of the living and nonliving things you will be studying in science. They include a list of facts about animals and a chart comparing and contrasting the planets of the solar system. There is also information about measurements and the metric system.

# Animal Facts

| Animal | Male | Female | Young | Group | Gestation (days) | Longevity (years) |
|--------|------|--------|-------|-------|------------------|-------------------|
| Bear | He-bear | She-bear | Cub | Sleuth | 180-240 | 18-20 (34)* |
| Cat | Tom | Queen | Kitten | Clutter/Clowder | 52-65 | 10-17 (30) |
| Cattle | Bull | Cow | Calf | Drove/Herd | 280 | 9-12 (25) |
| Chicken | Rooster | Hen | Chick | Brood/Flock | 21 | 7-8 (14) |
| Deer | Buck | Doe | Fawn | Herd | 180-250 | 10-15 (26) |
| Dog | Dog | Bitch | Pup | Pack/Kennel | 55-70 | 10-12 (24) |
| Donkey | Jack | Jenny | Foal | Herd/Pace | 340-385 | 18-20 (63) |
| Duck | Drake | Duck | Duckling | Brace/Herd | 21-35 | 10 (15) |
| Elephant | Bull | Cow | Calf | Herd | 515-760 | 30-60 (98) |
| Fox | Dog | Vixen | Cub/Kit | Skulk | 51-60 | 8-10 (14) |
| Goat | Billy | Nanny | Kid | Tribe/Herd | 135-163 | 12 (17) |
| Goose | Gander | Goose | Gosling | Flock/Gaggle | 30 | 25-30 |
| Horse | Stallion | Mare | Filly/Colt | Herd | 304-419 | 20-30 (50+) |
| Lion | Lion | Lioness | Cub | Pride | 105-111 | 10 (29) |
| Monkey | Male | Female | Boy/Girl | Band/Troop | 149-179 | 12-15 (29) |
| Rabbit | Buck | Doe | Bunny | Nest/Warren | 27-36 | 6-8 (15) |
| Sheep | Ram | Ewe | Lamb | Flock/Drove | 121-180 | 10-15 (16) |
| Swan | Cob | Pen | Cygnet | Bevy/Flock | 30 | 45-50 |
| Swine | Boar | Sow | Piglet | Litter/Herd | 101-130 | 10 (15) |
| Tiger | Tiger | Tigress | Cub | | 105 | 19 |
| Whale | Bull | Cow | Calf | Gam/Pod/Herd | 276-365 | 37 |
| Wolf | Dog | Bitch | Pup | Pack | 63 | 10-12 (16) |

\* ( ) Record for oldest animal of this type

Sun

Mercury

Venus

Earth

Mars

Jupiter

Saturn

# Our Solar System

There are thousands of galaxies in the universe. Our solar system is in the Milky Way Galaxy, which is 150,000 light-years in diameter. This galaxy contains nearly one trillion stars. Our solar system has only one star—the sun—and nine planets.

**Mercury** has the shortest year.

Uranus

**Venus** spins the slowest.

**Earth** supports life for plants, animals, and people.

**Mars** has less gravity than Earth.

**Jupiter** is the largest planet. It is more than 10 times bigger than Earth.

**Saturn** has seven rings. It also has the most moons—23.

Neptune

**Uranus** has the most rings—15.

**Neptune** is three times as cold as Earth.

**Pluto** is the smallest planet and the farthest from the sun.

Pluto

| | Sun | Moon | Mercury | Venus | Earth | Mars | Jupiter | Saturn | Uranus | Neptune | Pluto |
|---|---|---|---|---|---|---|---|---|---|---|---|
| **Number of Moons** | 9 planets | 0 | 0 | 0 | 1 | 2 | 16 | 23 | 15 | 8 | 1 |
| **Diameter (in Miles)** | 865,400 | 2,155 | 3,032 | 7,519 | 7,926 | 4,194 | 88,736 | 74,978 | 32,193 | 30,775 | 1,423 |
| **Length of One Day*** | 25 days | 27 days | 59 days | 243 days | 24 hours | 25 hours | 10 hours | 11 hours | 17 hours | 16 hours | 6 days |
| **Length of One Year*** | | 365 days | 88 days | 225 days | 365 days | 687 days | 12 years | 29 years | 84 years | 165 years | 248 years |
| **Average Distance to Sun*** | | 93 million miles | 36 million miles | 67 million miles | 93 million miles | 142 million miles | 484 million miles | 887 million miles | 1,784 million miles | 2,796 million miles | 3,666 million miles |
| **Surface Temperature* (Fahrenheit)** | 10,000° (surface) 27,000,000° (center) | lighted side 260° dark side -280° | -346° to 950° | 850° | -127° to 136° | -191° to -24° | -236° | -203° | -344° | -360° | -342° to -369° |
| **Weight of a 100-Pound Person*** | | 16 | 39 | 90 | 100 | 38 | 253 | 107 | 91 | 114 | 7 |

*Approximate numbers

# U.S. Measurements

Here are some basic units in the United States system of measurement.

## Length (how far)

1 inch (in.) _____ ····· one inch

1 foot (ft.) = 12 inches

1 yard (yd.) = 3 feet = 36 inches

1 mile (mi.) = 1,760 yards = 5,280 feet = 63,360 inches

## Weight (how heavy)

1 ounce (oz.)

1 pound (lb.) = 16 ounces

1 ton = 2,000 pounds = 32,000 ounces

## Capacity (how much something can hold)

1 teaspoon (tsp.)

1 tablespoon (tb.) = 3 teaspoons

1 cup (c.) = 16 tablespoons = 8 ounces

1 pint (pt.) = 2 cups = 16 ounces

1 quart (qt.) = 2 pints = 4 cups

1 gallon (gal.) = 4 quarts = 8 pints = 16 cups

# The Metric System

Even though the **metric system** is not the official system of measurement in the United States, it is used in science, medicine, and some other areas. This system of measurement is based on units of 10. Here are some common metric measures.

## Length (how far)

1 millimeter (mm) - *one millimeter*

1 centimeter (cm) = **10 millimeters** _____ *10 millimeters*

1 meter (m) = **100 centimeters = 1,000 millimeters**

1 kilometer (km) = **1,000 meters = 100,000 centimeters = 1,000,000 millimeters**

## Weight (how heavy)

1 gram (g)

1 kilogram (kg) = **1,000 grams**

## Capacity (how much something can hold)

1 milliliter (ml)

1 liter (l) = **1,000 milliliters**

# Improving
# Math Skills

When you think of **math**, what do you think of? Adding numbers? Counting change? Measuring with a ruler? Dividing something into equal parts?

Math is this and much more. Learning math is almost like learning a new language. Math has its own special words and symbols. Math also has its own skills and strategies. This chapter will help you understand the language and strategies of mathematics. At the end of the chapter, you will find all kinds of helpful charts and tables.

# Solving Basic Word Problems

Most of your math assignments include at least two or three **word problems.** The best way to solve word problems is to follow a process. That way you won't miss any important details. Here's a process to try:

## Four-Step Process

### Read the problem.

Be sure you understand all the parts. Look for any key words like "how many" or "in all."

### Decide what you need to do.

Do you have to add a series of numbers? Do you have to multiply or subtract? Do you have to do more than one thing—maybe add, then subtract?

### Solve the problem.

There may be more than one way to solve a problem. Page 357 shows you five strategies for figuring out the same problem. (Remember, show all of your work so you can check it later.)

### Check your answer.

Here are two ways to check: (1) You can do the problem again, only in a different way. (2) You can start with your answer and work backward. Let's say that your answer to a problem is 42. You multiplied 6 times 7 to get that answer. If you divide 42 by 6, you should get 7. Or if you divide 42 by 7, you should get 6.

# Sample Word Problem

## Read the problem.

Susan and her best friend, Maria, are making chocolate cookies for their soccer picnic. There will be 13 people at the picnic, including four parents. They want to give each person three cookies. How many cookies do they need to make?

## Decide what you need to do.

After reading the problem, you know that you are looking for a total number of cookies. You also know the basic numbers you have to work with: 13 people with 3 cookies each.

## Solve the problem.

Let's say you decide to **skip-count** by three, 13 times. (See the next page for other strategies.)

$$3, 6, 9, 12, 15, \ldots 39$$

## Check your answer.

To check your work, you decide to solve the problem in a different way. You make **tally marks** in 13 groups of three (/// /// /// . . . ). You then add up all of your marks. (Your work checks out. The girls need to make 39 cookies.)

# Five Problem-Solving Strategies

There are many different ways to solve a word problem. Five different strategies are given below. (The numbers are from the sample word problem on page 356.)

**Skip-count** by three, 13 times.

3, 6, 9, 12, 15, 18, 21, 24, 27, 30, 33, 36, 39

**Make tally marks.** Put three marks in a group, make 13 groups, and add up all the marks.

/// /// /// /// /// /// /// /// /// /// /// /// ///

**Estimate and check.**

**Estimate:** 36 cookies

**Check:** Divide 36 by 3, 3)̄36. The answer is 12. That's close! Three more cookies are needed, because there are 13 people, not 12. (36 + 3 = 39)

**Use cubes or other counters.** Make 13 groups of 3 counters. Then count them all.

**Write a math problem.** Multiply the number of people by the number of cookies each person would get.

$$\begin{array}{r} 13 \quad \text{people} \\ \times\ 3 \quad \text{cookies (each)} \\ \hline 39 \quad \text{cookies (total)} \end{array}$$

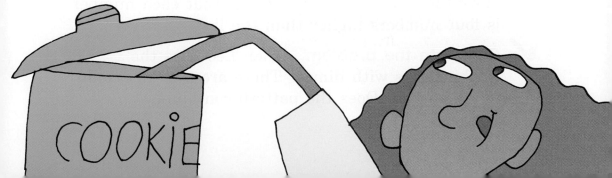

# Solving Brain Stretchers

Sometimes you are asked to do problems that can't be solved by simply multiplying or dividing the numbers. We call these types of problems **brain stretchers**. Your teacher may give you these problems to get you thinking. Here's such a problem:

> You shut your eyes and reach into a jar filled with pennies, nickels, and dimes. You pull out three coins. How much money might be in your hand?

# Problem-Solving Strategy

Let's see how one person works on this problem.

✔ Write equations. Leo starts by listing different coin combinations. (Each combination can be called an *equation*.)

> Pennies: **1¢ + 1¢ + 1¢ = 3¢**
> Nickels: **5¢ + 5¢ + 5¢ = 15¢**
> Pennies and Nickels: **1¢ + 1¢ + 5¢ = 7¢**
> **1¢ + 5¢ + 5¢ = 11¢**

✔ Organize a list or table. After Leo has all the penny and nickel combinations, he lists the totals from the smallest number to the largest: 3, 7, 11, 15.

✔ Look for a pattern. Leo notices that each number is four numbers higher than the last.

✔ Complete the problem. Then Leo tries the combinations with dimes. There are six. You could try them, too. Does the pattern continue?

# Symbols, Numbers, and Tables

Use the following symbols, tables, and charts whenever you need help with your math.

## Math Symbols

| | | |
|---|---|---|
| + plus (addition) | = is equal to | ° degree |
| − minus (subtraction) | ≠ is not equal to | % percent |
| × multiplied by | < is less than | ¢ cents |
| ÷ divided by | > is greater than | $ dollars |

# Addition and Subtraction Table

To add two numbers (8 + 6), find one of the numbers at the beginning of a row (8). Find your second number at the top of a column (6). Find your answer where the row and column meet (8 + 6 = 14).

To subtract two numbers (14 − 6), locate the larger number in the table (14). Then subtract the number at the top of the column (6). Your answer will be in the row to the far left (8).

| | 1 | 2 | 3 | 4 | 5 | 6 | 7 | 8 | 9 | 10 |
|---|---|---|---|---|---|---|---|---|---|---|
| 1 | 2 | 3 | 4 | 5 | 6 | 7 | 8 | 9 | 10 | 11 |
| 2 | 3 | 4 | 5 | 6 | 7 | 8 | 9 | 10 | 11 | 12 |
| 3 | 4 | 5 | 6 | 7 | 8 | 9 | 10 | 11 | 12 | 13 |
| 4 | 5 | 6 | 7 | 8 | 9 | 10 | 11 | 12 | 13 | 14 |
| 5 | 6 | 7 | 8 | 9 | 10 | 11 | 12 | 13 | 14 | 15 |
| 6 | 7 | 8 | 9 | 10 | 11 | 12 | 13 | 14 | 15 | 16 |
| 7 | 8 | 9 | 10 | 11 | 12 | 13 | 14 | 15 | 16 | 17 |
| 8 | 9 | 10 | 11 | 12 | 13 | 14 | 15 | 16 | 17 | 18 |
| 9 | 10 | 11 | 12 | 13 | 14 | 15 | 16 | 17 | 18 | 19 |
| 10 | 11 | 12 | 13 | 14 | 15 | 16 | 17 | 18 | 19 | 20 |

# Multiplication and Division Table

To multiply two numbers (4 × 6), find one of the numbers at the top of a column (4). Find the second number at the beginning of a row (6). Find your answer where the row and column meet (6 × 4 = 24). To divide (24 ÷ 6), find the larger number in the table (24). Then divide by the number at the far left (6). Your answer is at the top of the column (4).

|    | 0 | 1 | 2 | 3 | ④ | 5 | 6 | 7 | 8 | 9 | 10 |
|----|---|---|---|---|---|---|---|---|---|---|----|
| 0  | 0 | 0 | 0 | 0 | 0 | 0 | 0 | 0 | 0 | 0 | 0 |
| 1  | 0 | 1 | 2 | 3 | 4 | 5 | 6 | 7 | 8 | 9 | 10 |
| 2  | 0 | 2 | 4 | 6 | 8 | 10 | 12 | 14 | 16 | 18 | 20 |
| 3  | 0 | 3 | 6 | 9 | 12 | 15 | 18 | 21 | 24 | 27 | 30 |
| 4  | 0 | 4 | 8 | 12 | 16 | 20 | 24 | 28 | 32 | 36 | 40 |
| 5  | 0 | 5 | 10 | 15 | 20 | 25 | 30 | 35 | 40 | 45 | 50 |
| ⑥  | 0 | 6 | 12 | 18 | ㉔ | 30 | 36 | 42 | 48 | 54 | 60 |
| 7  | 0 | 7 | 14 | 21 | 28 | 35 | 42 | 49 | 56 | 63 | 70 |
| 8  | 0 | 8 | 16 | 24 | 32 | 40 | 48 | 56 | 64 | 72 | 80 |
| 9  | 0 | 9 | 18 | 27 | 36 | 45 | 54 | 63 | 72 | 81 | 90 |
| 10 | 0 | 10 | 20 | 30 | 40 | 50 | 60 | 70 | 80 | 90 | 100 |

# Roman Numerals

| | | | | | | | |
|----|---|------|----|------|----|---|-------|
| I | 1 | VII | 7 | XL | 40 | C | 100 |
| II | 2 | VIII | 8 | L | 50 | D | 500 |
| III | 3 | IX | 9 | LX | 60 | M | 1,000 |
| IV | 4 | X | 10 | LXX | 70 | | |
| V | 5 | XX | 20 | LXXX | 80 | | |
| VI | 6 | XXX | 30 | XC | 90 | | |

# Rounding Numbers

You can round a number to the nearest ten, hundred, thousand, or even million.

**Rounding to the Nearest Ten** ● If your number is 32, 32 is closer to 30 than to 40. So, 32 rounded to the nearest ten is 30.

**30**  31  (**32**)  33  34  35  36  37  38  39  40
◄••••••••••••••••••••••••••••••••••••••••••••

The number 36 is closer to 40 than to 30. So, 36 rounded to the nearest ten is 40.

30  31  32  33  34  35  (**36**)  37  38  39  **40**
••••••••••••••••••••••••••••••••••••••••••••►

Numbers ending in 1, 2, 3, or 4 are rounded down. Those ending in 6, 7, 8, or 9 are rounded up. And even though 5 is right in the middle, it is rounded up. So, 35 rounded to the nearest ten is 40.

30  31  32  33  34  (**35**)  36  37  38  39  **40**
••••••••••••••••••••••••••••••••••••••••••••►

# Skip-Counting

**Count by**

| | | | | | | | | | |
|---|---|---|---|---|---|---|---|---|---|
| **2's** | 2 | 4 | 6 | 8 | 10 | 12 | 14 | 16 | 18 | 20 |
| **3's** | 3 | 6 | 9 | 12 | 15 | 18 | 21 | 24 | 27 | 30 |
| **4's** | 4 | 8 | 12 | 16 | 20 | 24 | 28 | 32 | 36 | 40 |
| **5's** | 5 | 10 | 15 | 20 | 25 | 30 | 35 | 40 | 45 | 50 |
| **10's** | 10 | 20 | 30 | 40 | 50 | 60 | 70 | 80 | 90 | 100 |

## Place-Value Chart

| 7 | 5 | 2 | , | 8 | 4 | 3 |
|---|---|---|---|---|---|---|
| hundred thousands | ten thousands | thousands | , | hundreds | tens | ones |

| | |
|---|---:|
| **7** in the hundred thousands' place is | **700,000** |
| **5** in the ten thousands' place is | **50,000** |
| **2** in the thousands' place is | **2,000** |
| **8** in the hundreds' place is | **800** |
| **4** in the tens' place is | **40** |
| **3** in the ones' place is | **3** |

You read this six-digit number as **seven hundred fifty-two thousand eight hundred forty-three**.

# Fractions

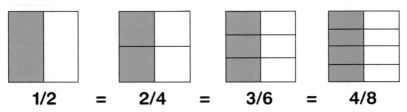

**1/2   =   2/4   =   3/6   =   4/8**

In 1/2, 1 is the numerator and 2 is the denominator. All the fractions above are called *equivalent fractions*. They all name the same part, or fraction, of the square . . . even though they have different numerators and denominators. Fractions with the same denominators are easy to compare.

**5/8 is greater than 3/8      1/4 is less than 3/4**

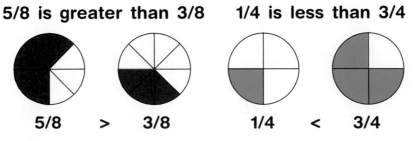

**5/8   >   3/8          1/4   <   3/4**

# Telling Time to the Minute

## 1:00 ·········▶

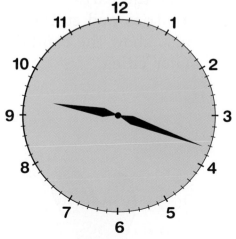

When the minute hand (long hand) is on 12, you write 00 for the minutes.

◀·············· **2:35**

When the minute hand is on a number, you can multiply that number by 5. See the multiplication table on page 360 if you have trouble counting by 5's. (5 × 7 = 35)

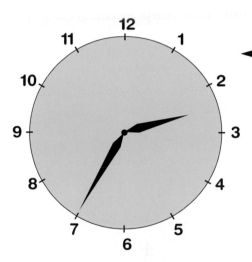

## 9:18 ···········▶

When the minute hand is between numbers, multiply the first number by 5. Then add the number of minute marks past that number. (3 × 5 = 15; 15 + 3 = 18)

# Using
# Maps

It's good to know more about the cities, countries, and bodies of water you hear about and read about. The section that follows will give you the map skills you need to find out about these places.

## Reading Maps

There are all kinds of **maps**—weather maps, maps that show the earth's surface, even maps that track satellites. Most of the maps in your handbook are *political maps*. Political maps show how the earth is divided into countries and states. They also show the capitals and major cities.

# Reading Maps

## Map Symbols

Mapmakers use special marks and symbols to show direction (north, east, south, and west). To the right is a *direction finder.* It will show you where north is. If a map does not have a direction finder, north is probably at the top of the page.

## The Legend

Important symbols are explained in a box printed on each map. This *legend,* or *key,* helps you understand and use the map. This map legend from the United States map includes symbols for state capitals, cities, and more.

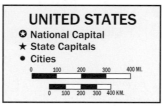

## The Map Scale

Legends also have a map scale. The *map scale* shows you how far it is between places. Here is the scale from the map of the United States. It uses inches.

**On Track** ▷ Line up the end of a ruler with the "0" on the scale. How many miles does one inch equal? (Your answer should be 400 miles.) What would two inches equal?

# Latitude and Longitude

**Latitude** ● The lines on a map that go from east to west around the earth are called lines of **latitude.** Latitude is measured in degrees, with the *equator* being 0 degrees (0°). Lines above the equator are called *north latitude.* Lines below the equator are called *south latitude.*

**Longitude** ● The lines on a map that run from the North Pole to the South Pole are lines of **longitude.** The north-south line measuring 0° passes through Greenwich, England. This line is called the *prime meridian.* Lines east of the prime meridian are called *east longitude.* Lines west of the prime meridian are called *west longitude.*

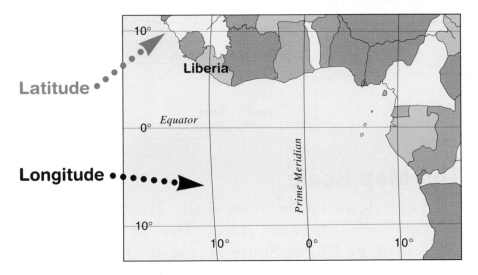

**Coordinates** ● The latitude and longitude numbers of a country or other place are called its *coordinates.* In each set of coordinates, latitude is written first, then longitude. In the map above, the African country Liberia is located at 7° N, 10° W.

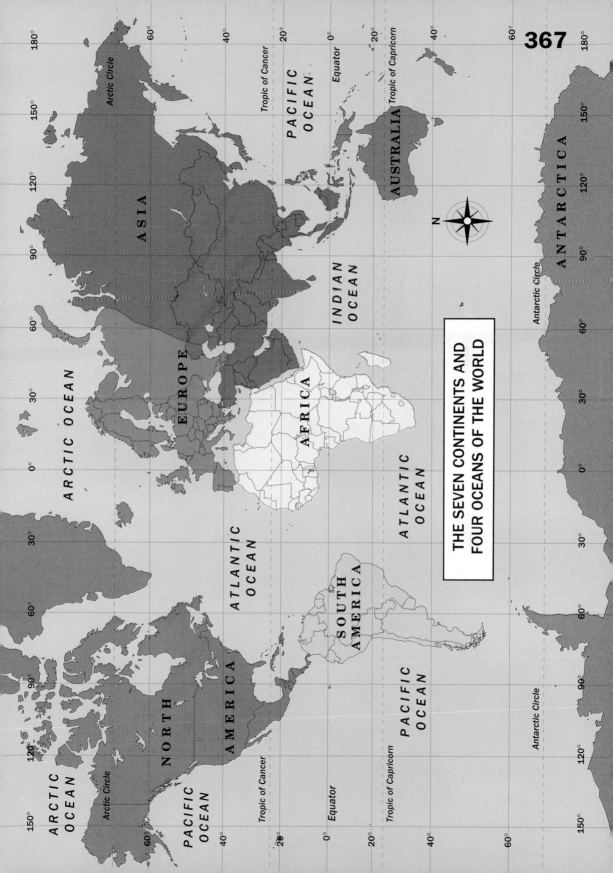

THE SEVEN CONTINENTS AND
FOUR OCEANS OF THE WORLD

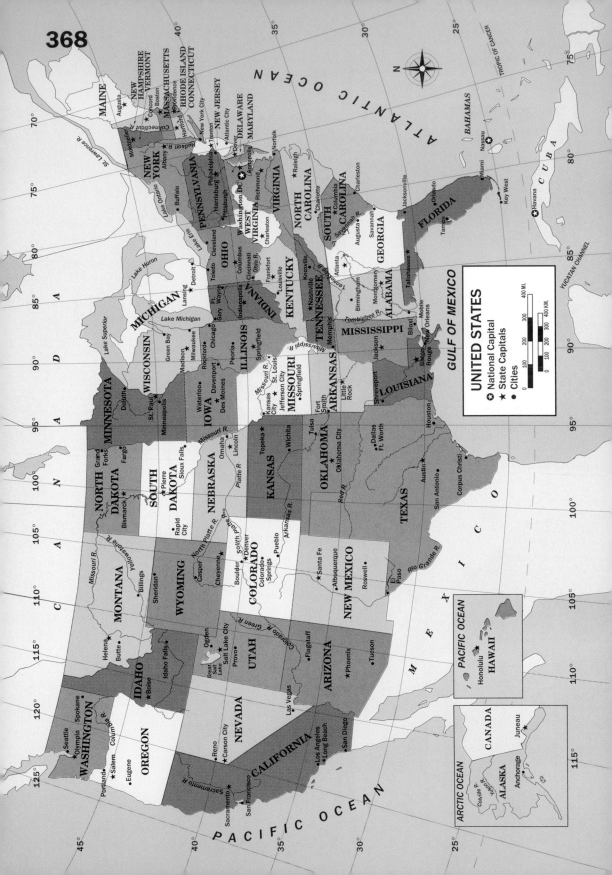

**368**

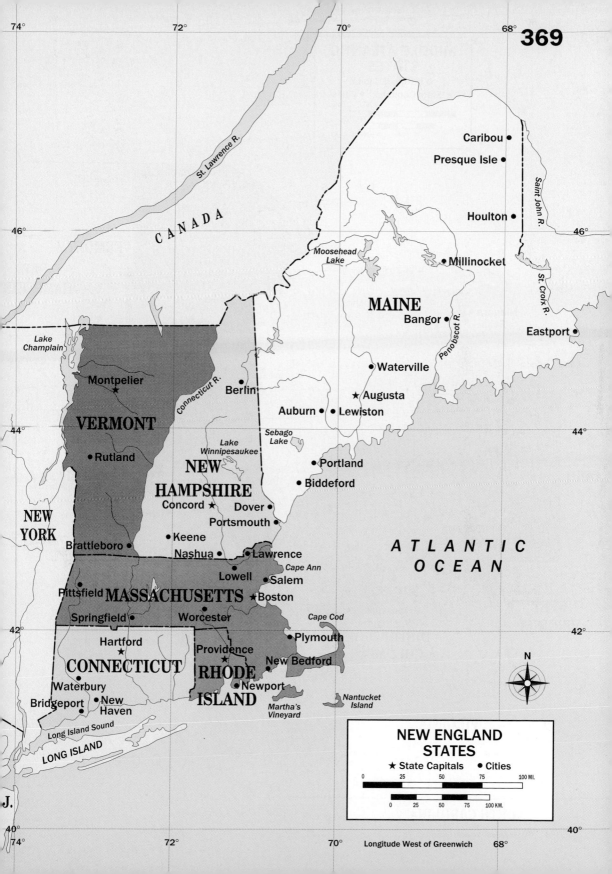

**NEW ENGLAND STATES**

★ State Capitals  • Cities

Longitude West of Greenwich

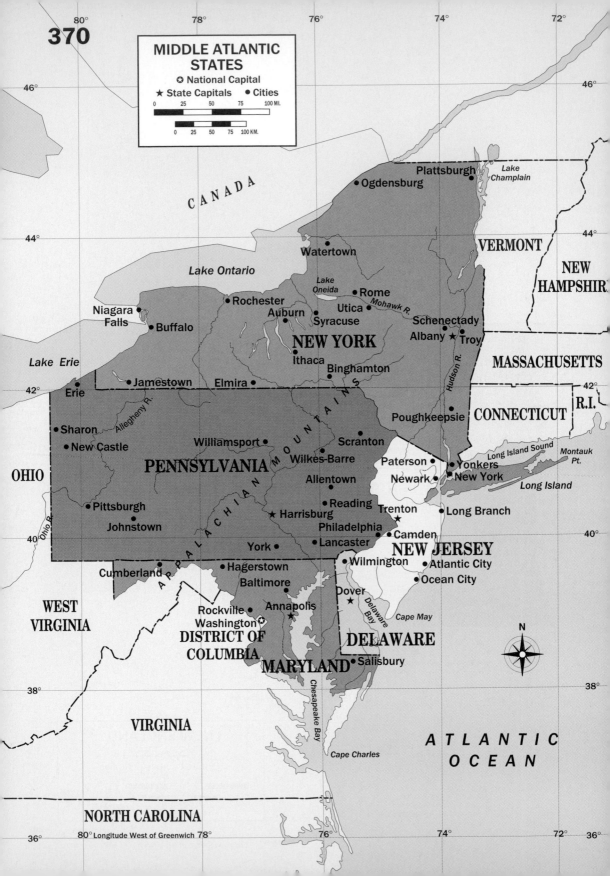

**370**

## MIDDLE ATLANTIC STATES

⊙ National Capital
★ State Capitals  • Cities

0  25  50  75  100 MI.

0  25  50  75  100 KM.

CANADA

Lake Ontario

**VERMONT**

Plattsburgh

Lake Champlain

Ogdensburg

**NEW HAMPSHIRE**

Watertown

Lake Oneida

Rome

Rochester

Auburn

Utica

Mohawk R.

Syracuse

Schenectady

**NEW YORK**

Albany ★ Troy

Niagara Falls

Buffalo

Ithaca

**MASSACHUSETTS**

Hudson R.

Lake Erie

Jamestown

Elmira

Binghamton

Erie

Poughkeepsie

**CONNECTICUT**

**R.I.**

Sharon

Allegheny R.

Scranton

Long Island Sound

Montauk Pt.

New Castle

Williamsport

Wilkes-Barre

Paterson

Yonkers

**OHIO**

**PENNSYLVANIA**

Allentown

Newark

New York

Long Island

APPALACHIAN MOUNTAINS

Pittsburgh

Reading

Trenton

Long Branch

Johnstown

★ Harrisburg

Philadelphia

Camden

Ohio R.

York

Lancaster

**NEW JERSEY**

Cumberland

Hagerstown

Wilmington

Atlantic City

**WEST VIRGINIA**

Baltimore

Dover ★

Ocean City

Rockville

Annapolis ★

Delaware Bay

Cape May

Washington ⊙

**DISTRICT OF COLUMBIA**

**DELAWARE**

**MARYLAND**

Salisbury

**VIRGINIA**

N

Chesapeake Bay

**ATLANTIC OCEAN**

Cape Charles

**NORTH CAROLINA**

80° Longitude West of Greenwich 78°

IOWA

LAKE ERIE

ILLINOIS     INDIANA     OHIO     PENNSYLVANIA

2°          88°          84°          80°          76°

40°                                              40°    N.J.

Wheeling

WEST          Washington          MD.     DEL.
VIRGINIA          DC

Frankfort          Charleston          VIRGINIA          Alexandria

Huntington

Ohio R.     Louisville     Lexington

MISSOURI          KENTUCKY          Lynchburg     James R.     Richmond

Paducah     Bowling Green          Roanoke          Newport     Norfolk
                                                              News
Kentucky          Cumberland R.          Winston-Salem     Greensboro     Roanoke R.
Lake
36°          Nashville     Knoxville                              Durham          36°
ARKANSAS     TENNESSEE                    NORTH     Raleigh
                    Chattanooga     Asheville     CAROLINA          Cape
                                        Charlotte                    Hatteras
Memphis                              Greenville     SOUTH
          Huntsville     Rome          Columbia     Wilmington
Mississippi R.          Athens          CAROLINA
          MISSISSIPPI          Atlanta          Myrtle Beach
Greenville          Birmingham               Augusta     Charleston
                    Tuscaloosa     GEORGIA     Savannah R.
32°               ALABAMA               Charleston          32°
Vicksburg     Jackson     Montgomery     Columbus
          Hattiesburg     Alabama R.               Savannah
Natchez                    ATLANTIC
          Mobile                         OCEAN
LOUISIANA     Biloxi     Pensacola          Jacksonville
          Tallahassee
          Panama City          Gainesville
                              FLORIDA
GULF OF                         Cape Canaveral
                              Orlando
MEXICO          Tampa
28°          St. Petersburg                    28°

                    Ft. Myers          West Palm Beach
          N          Lake
                    Okeechobee     Ft. Lauderdale
                    Naples          Miami

SOUTHEASTERN
STATES
✪ National Capital
★ State Capitals  • Cities
          Key West          BAHAMAS
          Florida Keys
0   50  100 150  200 MI.          Straits of Florida
0   50  100 150  200 KM.
24°                              Tropic of Cancer          24°

APPALACHIAN MOUNTAINS

APP... Chattahoochee R.

88° Longitude West of Greenwich  84°     CUBA     80°     76°

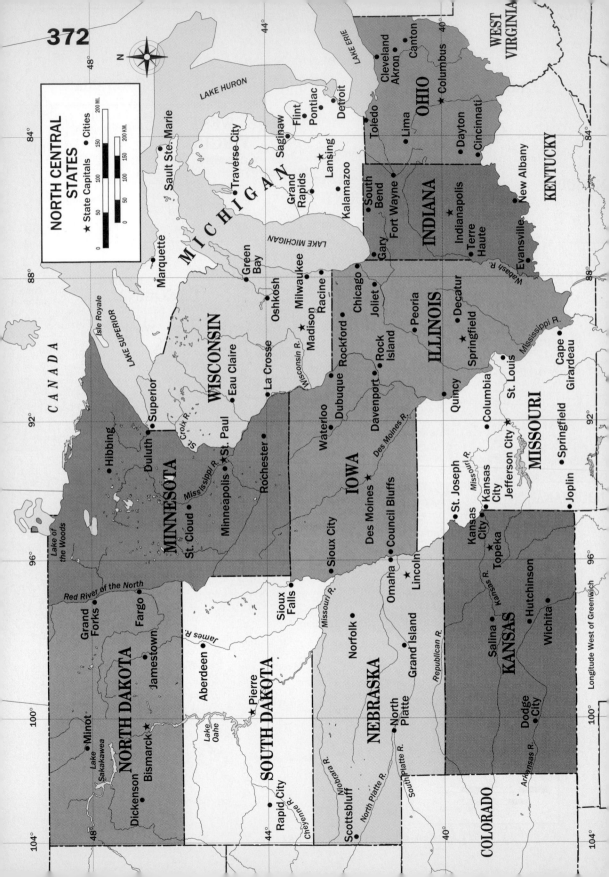

372

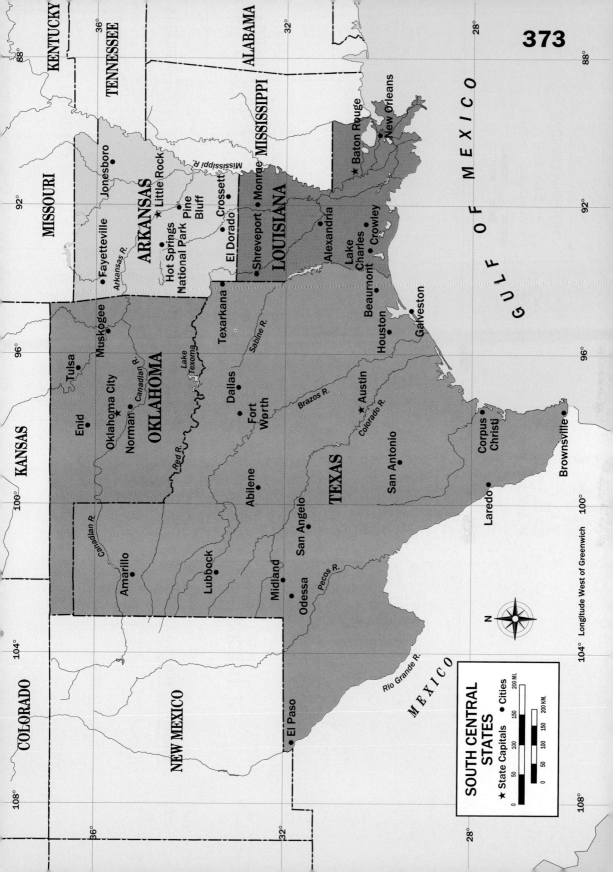

**373**

SOUTH CENTRAL
STATES

★ State Capitals    ● Cities

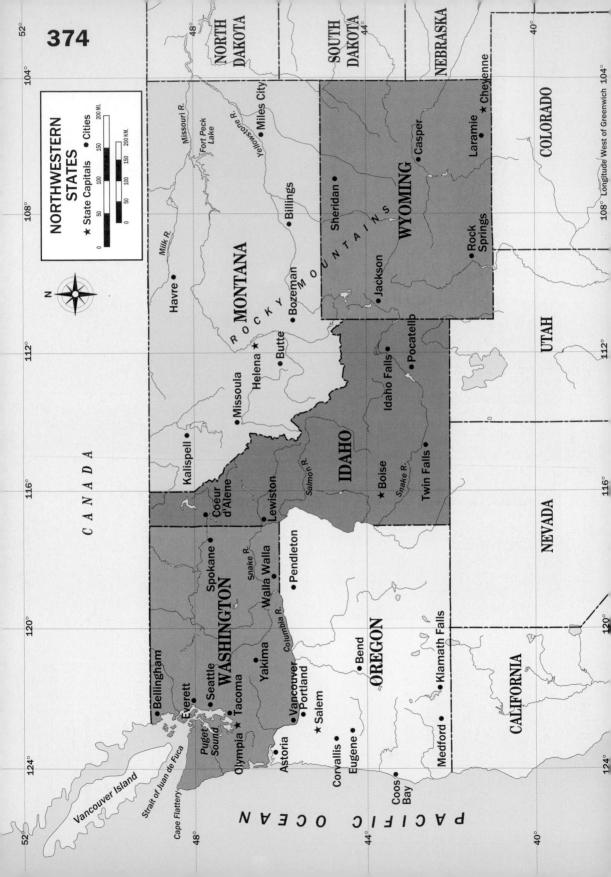

**374**

## NORTHWESTERN STATES

★ State Capitals  • Cities

200 Mi.
150
100
50
0

200 KM.
150
100
50
0

N

CANADA

**MONTANA**

Havre •
Milk R.
Missouri R.
Fort Peck Lake
Yellowstone R.
Miles City •
Billings •
Bozeman •
Butte •
★ Helena
Missoula •
ROCKY MOUNTAINS

**IDAHO**

Kalispell •
Coeur d'Alene •
Lewiston •
Salmon R.
Idaho Falls •
Pocatello •
★ Boise
Snake R.
Twin Falls •

**WYOMING**

Sheridan •
Jackson •
Casper •
Laramie •
★ Cheyenne
Rock Springs •

**WASHINGTON**

Bellingham •
Everett •
Seattle •
Tacoma •
★ Olympia
Spokane •
Yakima •
Walla Walla •
Pendleton •
Snake R.
Columbia R.

**OREGON**

Astoria •
★ Salem
Corvallis •
Eugene •
Portland •
Vancouver •
Bend •
Klamath Falls •
Medford •
Coos Bay •

Puget Sound
Strait of Juan de Fuca
Cape Flattery
Vancouver Island

NORTH DAKOTA
SOUTH DAKOTA
NEBRASKA
COLORADO
UTAH
NEVADA
CALIFORNIA

108° Longitude West of Greenwich 104°

**PACIFIC OCEAN**

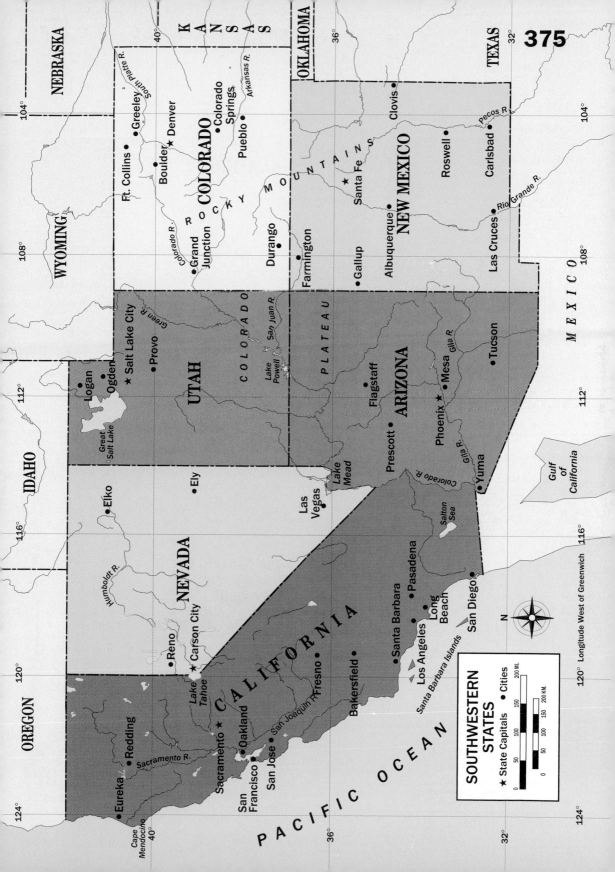

**375**

## SOUTHWESTERN STATES

★ State Capitals  • Cities

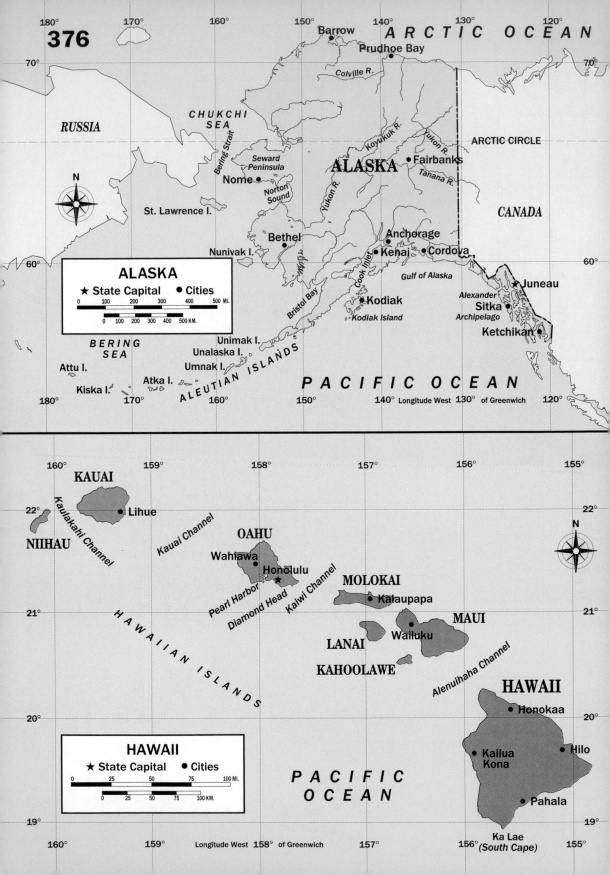

**376**

ARCTIC OCEAN

Barrow

Prudhoe Bay

Colville R.

70°

RUSSIA

CHUKCHI SEA

Bering Strait

ARCTIC CIRCLE

CANADA

Koyukuk R.

Yukon R.

ALASKA

Fairbanks

Tanana R.

Seward Peninsula

Nome

Norton Sound

Yukon R.

St. Lawrence I.

Bethel

Nunivak I.

Anchorage

Kenai

Cordova

60°

Cook Inlet

Gulf of Alaska

Juneau

Alexander Archipelago

Sitka

Ketchikan

### ALASKA
★ State Capital ● Cities

0 100 200 300 400 500 MI.

0 100 200 300 400 500 KM.

BERING SEA

Bristol Bay

Kodiak

Kodiak Island

Unimak I.

Unalaska I.

Umnak I.

Attu I.

Kiska I.

Atka I.

ALEUTIAN ISLANDS

PACIFIC OCEAN

Longitude West 140° 130° of Greenwich

---

## HAWAII

KAUAI

Lihue

NIIHAU

Kaulakahi Channel

Kauai Channel

OAHU

Wahiawa

Honolulu

Pearl Harbor

Diamond Head

Kaiwi Channel

MOLOKAI

Kalaupapa

MAUI

Wailuku

LANAI

KAHOOLAWE

HAWAIIAN ISLANDS

Alenuihaha Channel

HAWAII

Honokaa

Kailua Kona

Hilo

Pahala

Ka Lae (South Cape)

### HAWAII
★ State Capital ● Cities

0 25 50 75 100 MI.

0 25 50 75 100 KM.

PACIFIC OCEAN

Longitude West 158° of Greenwich

# Facts About the 50 States

| Largest U.S. Cities | Population |
|---|---|
| New York, NY | 8,008,278 |
| Los Angeles, CA | 3,694,820 |
| Chicago, IL | 2,896,016 |
| Houston, TX | 1,953,631 |
| Philadelphia, PA | 1,517,550 |
| Phoenix, AZ | 1,321,045 |
| San Diego, CA | 1,223,400 |
| Dallas, TX | 1,188,580 |
| San Antonio, TX | 1,144,646 |
| Detroit, MI | 951,270 |
| San Jose, CA | 894,943 |
| Indianapolis, IN | 781,870 |
| San Francisco, CA | 776,733 |
| Jacksonville, FL | 735,617 |
| Columbus, OH | 711,470 |
| Austin, TX | 656,562 |
| Baltimore, MD | 651,154 |
| Memphis, TN | 650,100 |
| Milwaukee, WI | 596,974 |
| Boston, MA | 589,141 |
| Washington, DC | 572,059 |
| El Paso, TX | 563,662 |
| Seattle, WA | 563,374 |
| Nashville-Davidson, TN | 545,524 |
| Charlotte, NC | 540,828 |

## LONGEST RIVERS

| | Length (Miles) |
|---|---|
| Mississippi | 2,340 |
| Missouri | 2,315 |
| Yukon | 1,979 |
| Rio Grande | 1,900 |
| Arkansas | 1,459 |
| Canadian | 1,458 |
| Colorado | 1,450 |
| Red | 1,290 |
| Columbia | 1,243 |
| Snake | 1,038 |

## LARGEST LAKES

| | Area (Sq. Mi.) |
|---|---|
| Lake Superior | 31,820 |
| Lake Huron | 23,010 |
| Lake Michigan | 22,400 |
| Lake Erie | 9,930 |
| Lake Ontario | 7,520 |
| Great Salt Lake (saltwater lake) | 1,800 |

## BOUNDARIES BETWEEN

**Alaska and Canada**
1,538 miles  (2,475 km)
**The 48 states and Canada**
3,987 miles  (6,416 km)
**The 48 states and Mexico**
1,933 miles  (3,111 km)

## DESERTS

| | Area (Sq. Mi.) |
|---|---|
| Mojave (CA) | 15,000 |
| Painted (AZ) | 7,000 |
| Great Salt Lake (UT) | 4,800 |
| Colorado (CA) | 2,500 |
| Black Rock (NV) | 1,000 |

# State Capitals and Nicknames

| STATE | CAPITAL | STATE NICKNAME |
| --- | --- | --- |
| Alabama | Montgomery | *Yellowhammer State* |
| Alaska | Juneau | *Land of the Midnight Sun* |
| Arizona | Phoenix | *Grand Canyon State* |
| Arkansas | Little Rock | *The Natural State* |
| California | Sacramento | *Golden State* |
| Colorado | Denver | *Centennial State* |
| Connecticut | Hartford | *Nutmeg State* |
| Delaware | Dover | *First State* |
| Florida | Tallahassee | *Sunshine State* |
| Georgia | Atlanta | *Peach State* |
| Hawaii | Honolulu | *Aloha State* |
| Idaho | Boise | *Gem State* |
| Illinois | Springfield | *Prairie State* |
| Indiana | Indianapolis | *Hoosier State* |
| Iowa | Des Moines | *Hawkeye State* |
| Kansas | Topeka | *Sunflower State* |
| Kentucky | Frankfort | *Bluegrass State* |
| Louisiana | Baton Rouge | *Pelican State* |
| Maine | Augusta | *Pine Tree State* |
| Maryland | Annapolis | *Free State* |
| Massachusetts | Boston | *Bay State* |
| Michigan | Lansing | *Wolverine State* |
| Minnesota | St. Paul | *Land of 10,000 Lakes* |
| Mississippi | Jackson | *Magnolia State* |
| Missouri | Jefferson City | *Show-Me State* |
| Montana | Helena | *Treasure State* |
| Nebraska | Lincoln | *Cornhusker State* |
| Nevada | Carson City | *Sagebrush State* |
| New Hampshire | Concord | *Granite State* |
| New Jersey | Trenton | *Garden State* |
| New Mexico | Santa Fe | *Land of Enchantment* |
| New York | Albany | *Empire State* |
| North Carolina | Raleigh | *Tarheel State* |
| North Dakota | Bismarck | *Peace Garden State* |

| STATE | CAPITAL | STATE NICKNAME |
|-------|---------|----------------|
| Ohio | Columbus | *Buckeye State* |
| Oklahoma | Oklahoma City | *Sooner State* |
| Oregon | Salem | *Beaver State* |
| Pennsylvania | Harrisburg | *Keystone State* |
| Rhode Island | Providence | *Ocean State* |
| South Carolina | Columbia | *Palmetto State* |
| South Dakota | Pierre | *Mount Rushmore State* |
| Tennessee | Nashville | *Volunteer State* |
| Texas | Austin | *Lone Star State* |
| Utah | Salt Lake City | *Beehive State* |
| Vermont | Montpelier | *Green Mountain State* |
| Virginia | Richmond | *The Old Dominion* |
| Washington | Olympia | *Evergreen State* |
| West Virginia | Charleston | *Mountain State* |
| Wisconsin | Madison | *Badger State* |
| Wyoming | Cheyenne | *Equality State* |

### HIGHEST POINT
Mt. McKinley, AK . . . . . . . . . . . . . . . . . 20,320 ft. (6,198 m)

### LOWEST POINT
Death Valley, CA . . . . . . . . . . 282 ft. below sea level (86 m)

### RAINIEST SPOT
Mt. Waialeale, Kauai, HI . . . 460-inch average annual rainfall

### DRIEST SPOT
Death Valley, CA . . . . . . . . 1.63-inch average annual rainfall

### HIGHEST WATERFALL
Yosemite, CA . . . . . . . . . . . . . . . . . . . . . .1,430 ft. (436 m)

**LARGEST STATE** . . . . . . . . . . . . . . Alaska 586,412 sq. mi.
**SMALLEST STATE** . . . . . . . . . . . Rhode Island 1,214 sq. mi.
**EASTERNMOST POINT** . . . . . . . . . . West Quoddy Head, ME
**NORTHERNMOST POINT** . . . . . . . . . . . . . Point Barrow, AK
**SOUTHERNMOST POINT** . . . . . . . . Ka Lae (South Cape), HI
**WESTERNMOST POINT** . . . . . . . . . . . . . Cape Wrangell, AK

# History in the Making

The **time line** in this chapter takes you on a trip through time . . . from 1492 when Columbus reached the West Indies, to 1969 when the first astronauts walked on the moon, to the present time.

For thousands of years before 1492, native people lived in America. The native people belonged to many different tribes and lived in five different regions. Each tribe had a special way of life related to the climate, animals, and landforms where they dwelled.

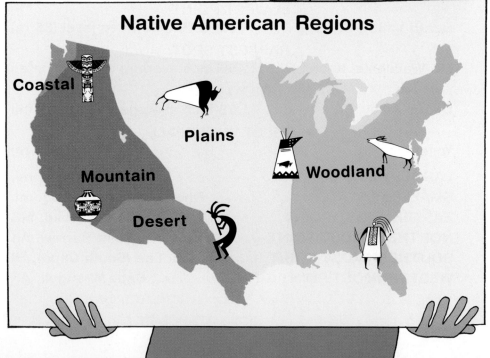

**Native American Regions**

Coastal

Plains

Mountain

Woodland

Desert

# A Closer Look

The historical time line on the next 10 pages covers more than 500 years of history. If you look closely, you'll see that the time line is divided into three parts:

**U.S. History** ••••••

**Science & Inventions** ••••

**Literature & Life** •••••••

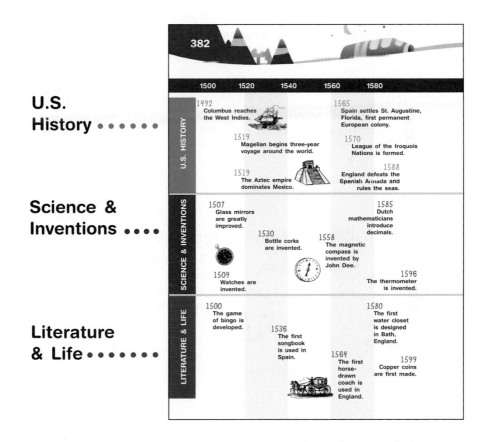

382

| 1500 | 1520 | 1540 | 1560 | 1580 |

**U.S. HISTORY**

1492 Columbus reaches the West Indies.

1519 Magellan begins three-year voyage around the world.

1519 The Aztec empire dominates Mexico.

1565 Spain settles St. Augustine, Florida, first permanent European colony.

1570 League of the Iroquois Nations is formed.

1588 England defeats the Spanish Armada and rules the seas.

**SCIENCE & INVENTIONS**

1507 Glass mirrors are greatly improved.

1530 Bottle corks are invented.

1558 The magnetic compass is invented by John Dee.

1585 Dutch mathematicians introduce decimals.

1509 Watches are invented.

1596 The thermometer is invented.

**LITERATURE & LIFE**

1500 The game of bingo is developed.

1536 The first songbook is used in Spain.

1564 The first horse-drawn coach is used in England.

1580 The first water closet is designed in Bath, England.

1599 Copper coins are first made.

As you use the time line, you can look at each of these three parts to see what was happening in the United States, in science, in literature, and in everyday life. Looking at history in this way will help you understand what life was really like back then.

**We hope you enjoy your travel through time!**

| 1500 | 1520 | 1540 | 1560 | 1580 |
|------|------|------|------|------|

## U.S. HISTORY

**1492**
Columbus reaches the West Indies.

**1519**
Magellan begins a three-year voyage around the world.

**1519**
The Aztec empire dominates Mexico.

**1565**
Spain settles St. Augustine, Florida, the first permanent European colony.

**1570**
League of the Iroquois Nations is formed.

**1588**
England defeats the Spanish Armada and rules the seas.

## SCIENCE & INVENTIONS

**1507**
Glass mirrors are greatly improved.

**1509**
Watches are invented.

**1530**
Bottle corks are invented.

**1558**
The magnetic compass is invented by John Dee.

**1585**
Dutch mathematicians introduce decimals.

**1596**
The thermometer is invented.

## LITERATURE & LIFE

**1500**
The game of bingo is developed.

**1536**
The first songbook is used in Spain.

**1564**
The first horse-drawn coach is used in England.

**1580**
The first water closet is designed in Bath, England.

**1599**
Copper coins are first made.

**1600**    **1620**    **1640**    **1660**    **1680**    **1700**

**1629**
**Massachusetts Bay Colony is established.**

**1607**
**England establishes Jamestown, Virginia.**

**1673**
**Marquette and Joliet explore the Mississippi River for France.**

**1619**
**The first Africans are brought to Virginia.**

**1682**
**William Penn founds Pennsylvania.**

**1620**
**Plymouth Colony is founded by Pilgrims.**

**1608**
**The telescope is invented.**

**1643**
**Evangelista Torricelli invents the barometer.**

**1680**
**The dodo, a large flightless bird, becomes extinct.**

**1629**
**Human temperature is measured by a physician in Italy.**

**1682**
**Halley's Comet is studied by Edmund Halley and named for him.**

**1609**
**Galileo makes the first observations with a telescope.**

**1689**
**Sir Isaac Newton describes gravity.**

**1609**
**The song "Three Blind Mice" is written.**

**1653**
**The first postage stamps are used in Paris.**

**1685**
**The first drinking fountain is used in England.**

**1658**
**The first illustrated book for children, *World of Visible Objects*, is written by John Comenius.**

**1630**
**Popcorn is introduced to Pilgrims by Native Americans.**

**1697**
***Tales of Mother Goose* is written by Charles Perrault.**

| 1700 | 1710 | 1720 | 1730 | 1740 |
|------|------|------|------|------|

## U.S. HISTORY

**1705**
The Virginia Act establishes public education.

**1707**
England (English) and Scotland (Scots) become Great Britain (British).

Scotland

England

**1718**
New Orleans is founded by France.

**1733**
The Molasses Act places taxes on sugar and molasses.

**1747**
The Ohio Company is formed to settle the Ohio River Valley.

## SCIENCE & INVENTIONS

**1709**
The pianoforte (first piano) is invented by Christofori Bartolommeo.

**1728**
The first dental drill is used by Pierre Fauchard.

**1735**
Rubber is found in South America.

**1742**
Benjamin Franklin invents the efficient Franklin stove.

## LITERATURE & LIFE

**1700**
*The Selling of Joseph* by Samuel Sewall is the first book against slavery of Africans.

**1704**
The first successful newspaper in the colonies, *Boston News-Letter*, is published.

**1726**
*Gulliver's Travels* is written by Jonathan Swift.

**1731**
Benjamin Franklin begins the first subscription library.

**1744**
John Newbery publishes the children's book, *A Little Pretty Pocket-Book*.

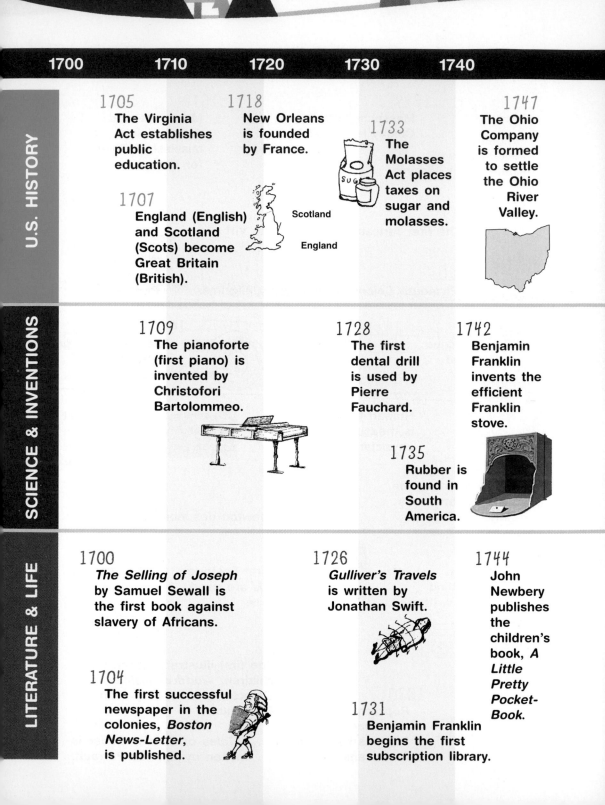

**1750**   **1760**   **1770**   **1780**   **1790**   **1800**

**1750**
Flatbed boats and Conestoga wagons begin moving settlers west.

**1765**
The Stamp Act tax is imposed on colonies by Britain.

**1776**
The Declaration of Independence is signed on July 4.

**1787**
The United States Constitution is signed.

**1781**
The British surrender October 19.

**1775**
First battles of the Revolutionary War are fought.

**1789**
George Washington is elected president.

**1752**
Benjamin Franklin discovers lightning is a form of electricity.

**1764**
The spinning jenny is invented for spinning cotton.

**1770**
The first steam carriage is invented.

**1783**
The first balloon is flown.

**1793**
Eli Whitney invents the cotton gin to take seeds out of cotton.

**1798**
Eli Whitney invents mass production.

**1752**
The first general hospital is established in Philadelphia.

**1765**
The first novel written for children is *Little Goody Two-Shoes*.

**1786**
The first ice-cream company in America begins production.

**1757**
Streetlights are installed in Philadelphia.

**1782**
The American bald eagle is first used as a symbol of the United States.

**1769**
Venetian blinds are first used.

**1795**
Food canning is introduced.

| 1800 | 1810 | 1820 | 1830 | 1840 |
|------|------|------|------|------|

## U.S. HISTORY

**1800**
Washington, D.C., becomes the U.S. capital.

**1804**
Lewis & Clark explore the Louisiana Territory and the Northwest.

**1819**
The U.S. acquires Florida from Spain.

**1836**
Texans defend Alamo.

**1838**
The Cherokee Nation is forced west on the "Trail of Tears."

**1848**
Gold is found in California.

**1830**
Native Americans are forced west by the Indian Removal Act.

## SCIENCE & INVENTIONS

**1800**
The battery is invented by Count Volta.

**1802**
The steamboat is built by Robert Fulton.

**1816**
The stethoscope is invented.

**1836**
Samuel Morse invents the telegraph.

**1846**
Elias Howe invents the sewing machine.

**1839**
The bicycle is invented by Kirkpatrick Macmillan.

## LITERATURE & LIFE

**1814**
Francis Scott Key writes "The Star-Spangled Banner."

**1816**
Niépce takes the first photograph.

**1804**
The first book of children's poems is published.

**1823**
*A Visit from St. Nicholas* is written by Clement Clark Moore.

**1834**
Louis Braille perfects a letter system for the blind.

**1835**
Hans Christian Andersen publishes *Tales Told to Children.*

**1849**
The safety pin is invented.

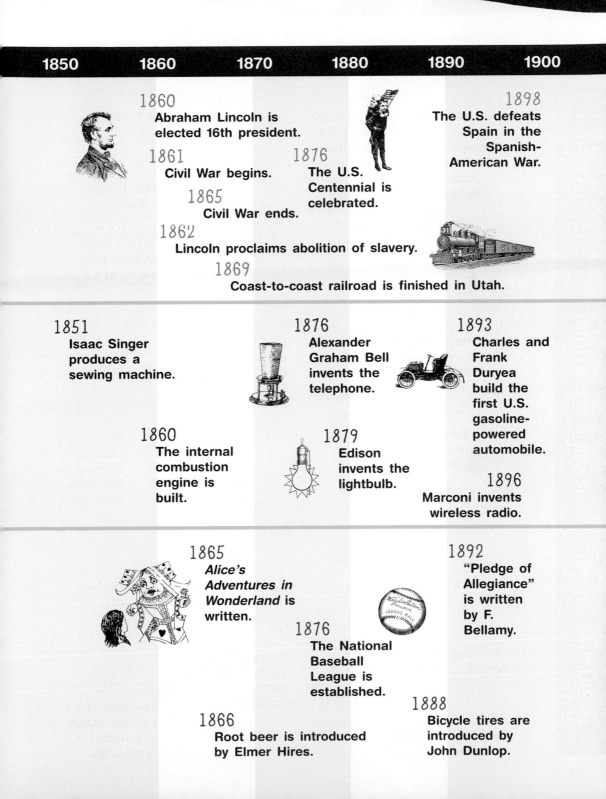

**1850**  **1860**  **1870**  **1880**  **1890**  **1900**

**1860**
Abraham Lincoln is elected 16th president.

**1861**
Civil War begins.

**1865**
Civil War ends.

**1862**
Lincoln proclaims abolition of slavery.

**1869**
Coast-to-coast railroad is finished in Utah.

**1876**
The U.S. Centennial is celebrated.

**1898**
The U.S. defeats Spain in the Spanish-American War.

**1851**
Isaac Singer produces a sewing machine.

**1860**
The internal combustion engine is built.

**1876**
Alexander Graham Bell invents the telephone.

**1879**
Edison invents the lightbulb.

**1893**
Charles and Frank Duryea build the first U.S. gasoline-powered automobile.

**1896**
Marconi invents wireless radio.

**1865**
*Alice's Adventures in Wonderland* is written.

**1876**
The National Baseball League is established.

**1866**
Root beer is introduced by Elmer Hires.

**1892**
"Pledge of Allegiance" is written by F. Bellamy.

**1888**
Bicycle tires are introduced by John Dunlop.

| 1900 | 1905 | 1910 | 1915 | 1920 |
|------|------|------|------|------|

## U.S. HISTORY

**1903**
Orville and Wilbur Wright fly the first successful airplane.

**1909**
The National Association for the Advancement of Colored People (NAACP) is founded.

**1917**
The United States enters World War I.

**1918**
World War I ends in Europe.

**1914**
The Panama Canal opens.

**1920**
Women gain the right to vote.

## SCIENCE & INVENTIONS

**1901**
Walter Reed discovers yellow fever comes from mosquitos.

**1904**
New York City develops a subway system.

**1913**
Henry Ford establishes an assembly line for automobiles.

**1915**
The coast-to-coast telephone system is established.

**1921**
Vaccine for tuberculosis is discovered.

**1922**
The electron scanner for television is developed.

## LITERATURE & LIFE

**1900**
The hot dog is created in New York City.

**1900**
*The Wonderful Wizard of Oz* is written by L. Frank Baum.

**1903**
The first World Series is played.

**1917**
*American Girl* magazine is published by the Girl Scouts.

**1913**
*Boy's Life* magazine is published by the Boy Scouts.

**1920**
The first radio station, KDKA, is founded in Pittsburgh.

1925　　1930　　1935　　1940　　1945　　1950

**1927**
Charles Lindbergh flies solo across the Atlantic Ocean.

**1933**
President Franklin Roosevelt begins the New Deal to end Great Depression.

**1941**
The U.S. enters World War II on Dec. 7.

**1945**
World War II ends.

**1945**
The United States joins the United Nations.

**1947**
Jackie Robinson becomes first black major league baseball player.

**1926**
Alexander Fleming develops penicillin.

**1938**
Modern-type ballpoint pens are developed.

**1935**
Radar is invented.

**1931**
The Empire State Building (102 stories, 1,250 feet) is completed as tallest in the world.

**1938**
The first photocopy machine is produced.

**1940**
Enrico Fermi develops the nuclear reactor.

**1925**
Potato chips are produced in New York City.

**1937**
*Snow White and the Seven Dwarfs* movie is made.

**1946**
*Highlights for Children* magazine is published.

**1931**
"The Star-Spangled Banner" becomes the U.S. national anthem.

**1928**
*My Weekly Reader* magazine is founded.

**1938**
Superman "Action Comics" are created.

| 1950 | 1955 | 1960 | 1965 | 1970 |
|------|------|------|------|------|

## U.S. HISTORY

**1950**
The United States enters Korean War.

**1959**
Alaska and Hawaii become states.

**1963**
President John F. Kennedy is assassinated.

**1969**
Neil Armstrong and Buzz Aldrin are the first men on the moon.

**1965**
U.S. troops are sent to Vietnam.

**1961**
Alan Shepard is the first U.S. astronaut in space.

**1954**
The Korean War ends.

**1968**
Martin Luther King, Jr., is assassinated.

## SCIENCE & INVENTIONS

**1957**
Russia launches first satellite, *Sputnik I.*

**1963**
Cassette music tapes are developed.

**1971**
Space probe *Mariner* maps the surface of Mars.

**1951**
Fluoridated water is discovered to prevent tooth decay.

**1958**
Stereo long-playing records are produced.

**1974**
Sears Tower (110 stories, 1,454 feet) is built in Chicago.

## LITERATURE & LIFE

**1950**
*Peanuts* comic strip is created by Charles Schulz.

**1957**
Theodor "Dr. Seuss" Geisel's *Cat in the Hat* is published.

**1964**
The Beatles appear on *The Ed Sullivan Show.*

**1951**
Fifteen million American homes have television.

**1969**
The *Sesame Street* television show begins.

**1957**
Elvis Presley is the most popular rock 'n' roll musician in the U.S.

**1975**     **1980**     **1985**     **1990**     **1995**     **2000**

**1975**
The Vietnam War ends.

**1981**
Sandra Day O'Connor becomes the first woman on the Supreme Court.

**1983**
Sally Ride becomes the first U.S. woman in space.

**1989**
The Berlin Wall is torn down.

**1991**
Persian Gulf War "Operation Desert Storm" begins.

**1994**
An earthquake rocks Los Angeles.

**1995**
Federal building bombed in Oklahoma City.

**2000**
More than 25 million people living in the U.S. were born in other countries.

**1976**
The *Concorde* becomes the world's first supersonic passenger jet.

**1983**
*Pioneer 10* space probe passes Neptune and leaves the solar system.

**1984**
Compact discs (CD's) are developed.

**1991**
Scientists report growing danger of hole in Earth's ozone layer.

**1991**
World Wide Web is launched.

**1997**
Scottish scientists clone an adult sheep.

**1976**
The United States celebrates its bicentennial.

**1976**
An earthquake in Tangshan, China, kills 240,000 people.

**1986**
Martin Luther King Day is proclaimed a national holiday.

**1987**
*The Whipping Boy* wins the Newbery Award.

**1988**
Thirty million U.S. schoolchildren have access to computers.

**1999**
The world's population reaches 6 billion.

**2000**
The last *Peanuts* comic strip is produced.

**1999**
The U.S. women's soccer team wins the World Cup.

# Index

The **index** helps you find information in your handbook. Let's say you want to learn how to write a haiku poem. You can look in your index under "haiku" or under "poetry" for help.

**Rambling** sentence, 73

**Reading,**
  Graphics, 195-199
  Mapping, 205
  Prefix, suffix, root, 201, 216-225
  Strategies, 200-206
  Vocabulary, 209-215

**Reading** journal, 79
**Realistic** stories, writing, 149-153
*Red/read,* 319
**Reference** books, 186
**Regular** verb, 331
**Repeating** sounds, 173
**Report,** classroom, 135-141
  Gathering grid, 138
**Resolution,** 119
**Response** sheet, writing, 49
**Response** to literature, 114-119
**Review,** book, 114-119
  Samples, 116-117
**Revising,** 13, 16, 41-44
  Checklist, 45
**Rhyme,** 173
*Right/write,* 319
*Road/rode/rowed,* 319
**Roman** numerals, 360
**Roots,** 201, 215, 216, 221-225 (list)
**Rounding** numbers, 361
**Run-on** sentence, 73

**Salutation,** 94, 128, 295, 298
**Science,** exploring, 348-353
**Scripting/scoring** a poem, 240
*Sea/see,* 320
**Search** engine, 191-192
*Seen/scene,* 320
**Selecting** subjects, 33-35

**Sensory** detail, 44
*Sent/scent/cent,* 317

**Sentences,** understanding, 322-325
  Combining, 74-75
  Fragment, 73
  Kinds of, 325
  Parts of, 72, 323-324
  Problems, 73
  Rambling, 73
  Run-on, 73
  Types of, 325

**Series,** words in a, 75, 295
**Setting,** 119, 207
**Sharing** in groups, 46-49, 280-283
**Short** talk, giving, 244-251
**Show,** don't tell, 44
**Sign** language, 344
**Signature,** letter, 94, 128
**Simile,** 173
**Simple,**
  Predicate (verb), 324
  Sentence, 325
  Subject, 323
**Singular** noun, 327
**Singular** verb, 331
**Skills,**
  Learning, 277-291
  Listening, 236-237
  Test-taking, 284-291
  Thinking, 263-275
  Viewing, 231-235
**Skip-counting,** 357, 361
*So/sew/sow,* 320
*Soar/sore,* 320
**Solar** system, 350-351
**Solution,** 207
**Solving** problems, 269
**Solving** word problems, 355-358
*Some/sum,* 320
*Son/sun,* 320
**Speech,** making a, 244-251
**Spelling,** 226-229